What People Are Saying About
Date, Love, Marry, Avoid

I'm usually a stoic sceptic, but Janine has a way of making this all make sense! If you've ever wondered why you're a good or not-so-good match with someone, this book will give you some great insights!
Shaa Wasmund, MBE

Janine's methodologies are a little unconventional but they absolutely work! Not in an exact science kind of way, but in an 'allowing you to self-reflect and make better decisions' kind of way. Working with her has helped me create more joy, become more intentional in life and grow as a person and an entrepreneur. Highly recommend Janine and her work.
Katya Varbanova, Viral Marketing Stars®

Janine is my go-to Chinese Astrologer and I consult her before making any major decisions in my life or business. If I were dating today, I would 100% ask Janine to check our charts for compatibility before committing.
Veronica Pullen, Online Marketing Strategist and Mentor

Date, Love, Marry, Avoid is a fun book. An amazing roadmap to finding love based on Chinese Astrology. A perfect guide to creating your fun and unique dating profile based on your animal. Put your animal on your dating profile to create intrigue. Just imagine talking about Chinese Astrology on your first date – how unique is that? My tiger husband and my pig are a perfect match; we were meant to be together.
Soni Pelty, Dating and Relationship Coach

Janine's work as a Chinese Astrologer is so very accurate. Wise and insightful, she also brings kindness and humour to her work. For seriously helpful insights into the dynamics of your relationship and its chance of loving success, you can do no better than work with Janine. She's the real deal.
Mary Hykel Hunt, Transformational Coach for life and business

I'm just a girl looking for love.
It was all getting a bit stressful online with all the dos and don'ts and the shoulds and should nots that it was taking all of the joy out of it. Until I found Janine's book. It actually confirmed who I was and that I could be exactly who I am and wanted to be and still find love. It makes it playful again. Thanks, Janine.
Kellie Blondel, Virtual Collaborative

Date, Love, Marry, Avoid

Find Your Soulmate

Date, Love, Marry, Avoid

Find Your Soulmate

Janine Lowe

BOOKS
Winchester, UK
Washington, USA

JOHN HUNT PUBLISHING

First published by O-Books, 2023
O-Books is an imprint of John Hunt Publishing Ltd., 3 East St., Alresford,
Hampshire SO24 9EE, UK
office@jhpbooks.com
www.johnhuntpublishing.com
www.o-books.com

For distributor details and how to order please visit the 'Ordering' section on our website.

Design: Lapiz Digital Services

UK: Printed and bound by CPI Group (UK) Ltd, Croydon, CR0 4YY
Printed in North America by CPI GPS partners

The author of this book does not dispense medical advice or
prescribe the use of any technique as a form of treatment for
physical, emotional, or medical problems without the advice of a
physician, either directly or indirectly. The intent of the author
is only to offer information of a general nature to help you in
your quest for emotional and spiritual well-being. In the event
you use any of the information in this book for yourself, which is
your constitutional right, the author and the publisher assume no
responsibility for your actions.

We operate a distinctive and ethical publishing philosophy in
all areas of our business, from our global network of authors to
production and worldwide distribution.

Contents

Introduction

Why did I write this book?

I've given so many readings and read so many charts that I've started to see a pattern to the way people fall in love – sometimes with the right person but so often with the wrong. I wanted to share my knowledge to help people to find the right person for them using Chinese astrology.

The dating market is huge right now because people want to meet the right person for them. Covid has reminded people how important the people and connections in their lives are. But how, in a world dominated by online communication and the shiny profiles of social media platforms, can we find our perfect match?

What if people had a roadmap to find them? What if they could recognise the personality types and characteristics that most matter to them and avoid investing time in someone they're unlikely to be compatible with.

I decided to write the book that I couldn't find on the market. I love helping people find their way in relationships and life, but I can only share so much in my one-to-one sessions and private groups. I wanted to write a book to give everyone a chance to find their partner based on thousands of years of research.

This book will tell you about the Chinese zodiac, the 12 animals and how to work out which one you are. Then you'll find out about yourself and how well you will match with each of the other signs. If you're tired of spending time trying to work out whether your potential partners are compatible with you and what's important to you, Chinese astrology will help.

This is a fun book you can share with your friends. You'll learn so much about yourself and may understand yourself and the influence of those stars when you were born in a way that you never have before.

Why me?

I've always been intuitive, and it got me into a lot of trouble as a child. My mum really struggled with it. Once she took me to see a religious person she knew. I was so lucky he understood me, but he advised me to hide my gift. It was so hard. I had to close myself down to hide who I was and that made me so unhappy.

Getting married to a man who wasn't afraid of who I really was gave me the chance to be myself again. I went back to knowing the phone would ring, before it did, and giving advice for the future which, though it seemed random, would turn out for the best. People often called me a witch. I was happy with that, even as a kid, because I loved Samantha from *Bewitched*.

It became obvious to me that I wasn't designed for a 9-5 job. I really wanted to use what I was good at as a career. A lovely friend suggested Feng Shui. I trained with various masters and became a Feng Shui consultant. Meeting people and being able to transform their lives in such a positive way has brought me such joy and fulfilment.

Then I found Chinese Astrology and Joey Yap. He became my mentor and taught me about metaphysics. This transformed my life. I became one of Joey Yap's affiliates in 2016 and, from him, I've learned to work with dates and times to create wealth for my clients and myself.

My business, both in Feng Shui and Chinese Astrology, has grown significantly. I consult with individuals and businesses on both. I've developed several successful bundle products which change according to the dates and times of the year.

Why Chinese Astrology?

Looking to the stars to find our soulmate isn't new. People have been using the stars for insight into their strengths and weaknesses and how to use them to be happy, healthy, and wealthy for thousands of years.

Most of us in the Western world are familiar with the Western zodiac. A lot of science has gone into the mapping of the stars at the time of our birth and what influence that would have on different parts of our lives. Whether you are a Gemini or a Libra you probably have at least a basic understanding of the characteristics of your 'sign'.

But are you familiar with the Chinese zodiac? The Chinese have a strong link with the metaphysical world and have been studying astronomy and astrology, Feng Shui and other sciences for thousands of years.

In fact, Chinese astrology came about during the Han dynasty which ran from 206 BC to 220 AD. That's 206 years before the birth of Christ. They were mapping the stars and the position of the stars and planets to determine the characteristics, strengths and weaknesses of people based on when they were born. This was all happening around the same time as astronomy was being studied all over the world.

The Chinese have a long, proud history and throughout the dynasties that ruled the country before the current regime, they focused a lot on science and medicine. Most of you will have heard of Acupuncture, Feng Shui and the Chinese zodiac animals – just some of the results of that focus. These days people are even more focused on finding their life partner, since Covid has made us reassess our lives and what is really important to us. For many, our connections with people who matter to us and we want to share our lives with has become a major priority again. Have you considered using it to find your perfect match?

Let me tell you some more about it. Don't worry, you're not going to need a PhD in astrology or astronomy to understand it! Fortunately, after working with the Chinese zodiac for so many years I can keep it to what you really need to know.

Not dissimilar to Western astrology, Chinese astrologers worked out that elements of a person's character and destiny could be determined by the position of the planets, the sun and the moon at the time you were born. These very patient astrologers watched as the planets made their way around the sun, and putting everything they had observed together, they developed a system to forecast the destiny of people based on their birth date and where the key planets, the sun and the moon were at that point in time. The year, month, day and hour all help determine our personal character and this system is still used today.

Chinese astrology is much more influenced by the moon, than by the sun. Whereas many of us may be aware of our 'sun sign' under Western astrology – the Chinese year from an astrology point of view doesn't even start until after the first new moon of the year which is usually between 21st January and 20th February every year.

So, as we've established, without disappearing down the rabbit hole that is the serious astrological and astronomical data and research that these are based on, there are 12 signs. It's believed that these animals were first recorded in the Zhan Guo period which goes back as far as 5th century BC, but no date has been recorded. The animals are:

- Rat
- Ox
- Tiger
- Rabbit
- Dragon
- Snake
- Horse
- Goat
- Monkey
- Rooster
- Dog
- Pig

There are quite a few legends as to how they came to appear in the order that they do. They are too fun not to include two here.

It's said that Buddha invited the animals to race for their place in the zodiac. It is said that the Tiger was sleeping and missed the race altogether, and his friend the Rat chose not to wake him. The Rat sped through the race but reached a river and couldn't cross. Just as the Rat was wondering how to cross, the benevolent Ox turned up and the Rat convinced him to give him a ride on his back. The Ox agreed and on the other side the Rat jumped off and beat his new friend to the first place. It is said that the Tiger never forgave his friend for not waking him up.

Another legend relates to the Jade Emperor who wanted to choose 12 animals to be his guards. He sent a message to the world that these 12 animals would be chosen according to what order they came through Heavenly Gate; the earlier they entered, the earlier they would appear in the zodiac.

Of course, the explanation for the order the animals appear in has much more to do with the characteristics of those born under the influences of the celestial bodies the Chinese base them on. The characteristics determine what happens in life.

Let's talk about just a few of these characteristics:

Rats are intellectual, charismatic, sociable, artistic, and sensitive.

Oxen are ambitious, dependable, patient, and methodical.

Tigers are passionate, impulsive, affectionate, and humanitarian.

Rabbits are graceful, sensitive, homemaking, caring and loving.

Dragons are attractive, flamboyant, ambitious, and intuitive.

Snakes are intuitive, philosophical, intelligent, and sexy.

Horses are sexy, talented, sociable, and enthusiastic.

Goats are talented, romantic, gentle and friendly.

Monkeys are witty, entertaining, hardworking and loving.

Roosters are charming, astute, brave, sociable and fashionable.

Dogs are sensitive, methodical, honest and intelligent.

Pigs are charitable, caring, virtuous and amusing.

How can you work out which animal sign you are?

It's simple. Really!

1. First step – what year were you born?
2. Second step – what date was the Chinese New Year on the year you were born? A very quick Internet search will answer that for you.
3. Third step – if your birthday was before the Chinese New Year then you will be the sign of the previous year. If it was after, then you will be the sign for that year.

Let's look at an example:

If you were born on 20th June 1968, you are a Monkey. But if you were born on 15th January 1968, you would be a Goat, because 15th January was before the Chinese year in 1968.

Let's look at what years apply to which signs, so you can see what sign you are. Remember if you were born before the Chinese New Year in each of these years you will be the sign of the year before.

Rat	1912, 1924, 1936, 1948, 1960, 1972, 1984, 1996, 2008, 2020
Ox	1913, 1925, 1937, 1949, 1961, 1973, 1985, 1997, 2009, 2021
Tiger	1914, 1926, 1938, 1950, 1962, 1974, 1986, 1998, 2010, 2022

Rabbit	1915, 1927, 1939, 1951, 1963, 1975, 1987, 1999, 2011, 2023
Dragon	1916, 1928, 1940, 1952, 1964, 1976, 1988, 2000, 2012, 2024
Snake	1917, 1929, 1941, 1953, 1965, 1977, 1989, 2001, 2013, 2025
Horse	1918, 1930, 1942, 1954, 1966, 1978, 1990, 2002, 2014, 2026
Goat	1919, 1931, 1943, 1955, 1967, 1979, 1991, 2003, 2015, 2027
Monkey	1920, 1932, 1944, 1956, 1968, 1980, 1992, 2004, 2016, 2028
Rooster	1921, 1933, 1945, 1957, 1969, 1981, 1993, 2005, 2017, 2029
Dog	1922, 1934, 1946, 1958, 1970, 1982, 1994, 2006, 2018, 2030
Pig	1923, 1935, 1947, 1959, 1971, 1983, 1995, 2007, 2019, 2031

Let's look at another example:

If you were born in July 1998, you would be a Tiger, but if you were born on 10th January 1998 you were born under the sign of the Ox.

But there's more...

So, if you were born in August 2002 after the first new moon you are a Horse and you're sexy, talented, sociable and enthusiastic.

However, that's not the whole story. The month, day, and hour you were born also impact your character and destiny.

These 4 elements – year, month, day and hour – are known as the 'pillars of destiny' or Ba Zi.

Year	Outer animal: what you manifest outwardly to the world around you and your relationships with friends and family.
Month	Inner animal: less obvious characteristics that you possess but rarely share with others and your relationship with your career and mentors.
Day	True animal represents who you will grow into as an adult and the relationship between you and your partner.
Hour	Secret animal, who you are at your very core – your truest nature and your relationships with your children and wealth.

So, let's use a pretend person, 'Imogen'. 'Imogen' was born at 9.35pm on Monday 2nd August 2002. I have no idea whether 2nd August 2002 was a Monday but let's pretend that it was just for this example. If you want to know what day you were born – you can do an Internet search and find out.

We already know that Imogen is a Horse based on the year she was born. So, she appears to the world to be sexy, talented, sociable, and enthusiastic. There is no downside to that! The year she was born in, as a Horse, influences her relationship with friends and family.

Let's look at the month she was born – August.

Here are the signs that apply to each of the months of the year:

January	Ox	July	Goat
February	Tiger	**August**	**Monkey**
March	Rabbit	September	Rooster
April	Dragon	October	Dog
May	Snake	November	Pig
June	Horse	December	Rat

The month you're born in refers to your less obvious characteristics and personality. Those you don't necessarily share with others. Imogen's inner characteristics, less likely to be seen by the world, include being witty, entertaining, hardworking, and loving.

The day she was born also tells us something about Imogen. It tells us who she will grow into as an adult and the relationship between her partner and herself.

Monday	**Goat**
Tuesday	Dragon
Wednesday	Horse
Thursday	Rat, Pig
Friday	Rabbit, Snake and Dog
Saturday	Ox, Tiger and Rooster
Sunday	Monkey

Imogen as she grows and develops will become talented, romantic, gentle and friendly.

Her final influence Ba Zi influences down to the hour she was born. This number refers to the purest and truest core of yourself. This is who Imogen is under all of the layers, and different faces she shows to others around her. It also influences her relationship with her children.

1am – 3am	Ox
3am – 5am	Tiger
5am – 7am	Rabbit
7am – 9am	Dragon
9am – 11am	Snake
11am – 1pm	Horse
1pm – 3pm	Goat
3pm – 5pm	Monkey
5pm – 7pm	Rooster
7pm – 9pm	Dog
9pm – 11pm	**Pig**
11pm – 1am	Rat

Born at 9.35pm the core of Imogen, her truest nature is a Pig. At the heart of herself she is charitable, caring, virtuous and amusing.

Imogen, therefore, has the following 4 pillars of destiny, all playing their part in her life:

1. Horse
2. Monkey
3. Goat
4. Pig

Each of these will influence her development and destiny.

Why don't you use these tables to work out your four pillars? Remember that it's not unusual for us to have the same animal show up more than once in your four pillars. So, your year and hourly pillar could both be Horse or Goat, for example.

There's more…

The Elements

If that doesn't make you feel like a fascinating and complex character already then there is another layer that provides extra challenges and talent: they are the elements. Critically for those of you reading this to find your other half, this can also help determine whether you are going to gel or clash with other signs.

You've heard of Yin and Yang. This is important to cover at this point in the book. We are all pretty much a mix of both, ideally. However, thanks to our birth we tend to be more one than the other.

Yin types are more intuitive and introverted and Yang people are often more extroverted and logically minded.

Back to the 5 elements which are Wood, Fire, Earth, Metal and Water.

Each of the animal signs fall into one of the elements:

- Earth: Ox, Dragon, Dog, Goat
- Metal: Rooster, Monkey
- Wood: Rabbit, Tiger
- Fire: Horse, Snake
- Water: Rat, Pig

Let's look at some of the qualities these elements bring to the party.

Metal

Strength is one of the greatest qualities of metal types. They are not easily swayed or bent to another's will. You are tough! However, there are some challenges – it's not unusual for your perseverance to have its downsides – like becoming a workaholic. You're very focused and confident and will usually achieve what you set out to.

Water

You are flexible and adaptable. You can either be impatient, pushy, and wanting to move forward fast or you can be calm and peaceful and literally go with the flow.

Wood

The idea of wood people is that you always grow upward towards the sky. You move upwards naturally. You're generous souls and you're solid.

Fire

You're dynamic and enthusiastic and passionate. But you can be aggressive.

Earth

You are stable, patient, and responsible. You can move slowly though, while steadfast, this can frustrate those who are faster – the movers and shakers in the world.

Which signs are the luckiest?

Everyone asks me this, but the truth is that all of the animal signs are lucky and have special abilities in different areas. We'll cover this in much more detail in the chapters on your sign but here are some great examples.

Given that we are talking about love in this book I'll tell you that Horses, Rats, Roosters and Rabbits are referred to by Chinese astrologers as peach blossoms, which means they are the lucky in love animals. People just can't help falling in love with them and they don't even know why. They just have a bit of magic in their pockets. Their best months for love are December, March, June and September.

Whereas Pigs, Monkeys and Tigers are the wealth animals. February, August, and November are their best months to attract extra money. There are also particular wealth days every 12 days or so, which a Chinese astrologer can identify for you.

Dragons and Snakes are blessed with intuition. They are all-knowing. Their most powerful months are April and May and, in those months, everyone has a chance to tap into their intuition.

Oxen and Goats are the most noble and wise souls. They are the people everyone else wants to turn to for advice. Their strongest months are January and July, when they can tap into their innate wisdom most strongly.

Before we move to your best love matches, I'm guessing you'll want to know what colours to wear on your first date with your potential significant other, to bring you luck in love. Each sign has colours associated with it that will bring out the best in you.

Rat	Blue and black
Ox	Earthy colours
Tiger	Blue and green
Rabbit	Blue and green
Dragon	Red and purple
Snake	Orange and red
Horse	Red and orange
Goat	Pink and yellow
Monkey	Greys and whites
Rooster	Silver and Gold
Dog	Burgundy and tangerine
Pig	Blue and white

At last, it's time to talk about who you'd be best to date, love, marry or avoid...

Rat

The first sign in the Chinese Horoscope is the Rat.

At first sight:

Rat years	You were born after the Chinese New Year in: 1900, 1912, 1924, 1936, 1948, 1972, 1984, 1996, 2008 or, if you are very young, 2020.
Rat months	Your love mojo is going to be highest in April, August and December. From 6th December and 5th January, you are going to be on fire!
Rat days	Dust off your best dating gear on Thursdays.
Rat hours	As a night owl you are hottest between 11pm and 1am.
Element	Water

Top traits	You are one of the four signs that is super lucky in love. If that wasn't enough, you're blessed with great looks. You're a super sociable soul with charisma in spades. And it's not just all of the extrovert stuff you've got going for you – you can be one of the more sensitive lovers amongst the Chinese animal signs.
How you're likely to appear on your first date	You're attractive and look fit in a quirky, individual style.
Best colours	You'll rock blue, white and grey, but ditch the red it will kill the mood.
Lucky number	Your best number is 1 but 9 just isn't going to work for you.
Lucky direction	Happy days your best directions are Northeast & Southeast. South isn't the direction you want to be heading.

If you're a Rat then the great news is that you are one of the four signs in Chinese astrology most likely to be lucky in love, but before we get into that let's talk about you.

Rats come across as being completely extroverted. You can't stop talking, but there is an introvert hidden in there as well. You probably don't need to be told this but you were the one at school who couldn't stop chatting and chances are that's what you were most in trouble for; you just don't know when to shut up. You always had your hand up even when you didn't listen to the question first. You're the veritable 'ants in your pants' sign of the Chinese zodiac.

You're super-opinionated. You won't need to be told this. Despite your endless opinions on everything, you won't always have the facts to hand. That mouth of yours will have gotten you into trouble, probably since you were a kid. You're outspoken, but the good news is that there are signs who will be totally cool with that. You like to think you know everything, that is the flavour of the personality. You just like to know more than other people or at least appear to.

You might be outspoken, but Rats are sensitive souls. You can be sarcastic and knock people, but don't realise when you hurt someone. You are never nasty. You rarely have a filter on your mouth, and you're used to expressing yourself freely right from childhood.

Rats are blessed with strong intuitive senses. You can talk to each other intuitively and at a deeper level. When someone is in flow with you, you'll both laugh a lot. You'll be the one carrying the conversation, so you will need strong characters around you. When everyone else at the dinner table is eating, you won't have touched your food because you'll be too busy chatting.

You're totally into the 'wine, (wo)men and song'. A socialite who loves to drink and dance all night. You make great DJs. You're hugely into sex with the right person. Contact is critical to Rats. You don't always need to get down to 'the business' but there will need to be a lot of touching and cuddles. If you're not getting any you're going to be moody and, if you'll excuse the pun, 'touchy'. All of you Rats will have struggled during Covid if you've had no human contact; it will have made you feel very, very low. I've yet to meet a Rat who doesn't want to be in a relationship. Rats don't like to be alone. If you find yourself alone, you'll always have the TV or music on.

As you start your partying years you might find you're drawn to drugs, alcohol and cigarettes. You're the one who might take up smoking because you want to lose weight.

At social events you'll be the one standing back with your fag in your mouth, wishing you were eating the food and judging those who are the first at the table. You'll be thinking 'look at me, I'm not eating'. You want to eat but you want to be stick thin more than you want the food. You know I'm right – you're quietly judging those who dare to eat in public.

Rats do love food and it's not unusual to find your people in the hospitality industry. But trust me, you won't be eating your own food. If you are eating, then it will be in secret because you won't want anyone to realise you actually do eat.

Ironically Rats do NOT like exercise. You might have a Dog, rather than a cat, because you like the outdoors, and a walk is much more fun than a gym. Swimming in the sea is fine, because you're an outdoor type, but there would have to be a very good reason to get you into a pool, or it would be far too boring and not fun or 'hippyish' enough. You need to be free and will always choose to be outdoors. Even at the beach you'll be carrying the surfboards or windsurfers – you like to 'do' things. It needs to be fun, and you never exercise just for the sake of it. You quite like gardens and you're good at it. But you'll need to know all of the full and correct names for your plants – you know, the long, Latin-sounding ones.

You're likely to have multitudes of children, stop, then have more. You're going to either be completely career-oriented or a stay-at-home parent. There's no in-between. Trying to balance both won't work for you, because you like to be the best at what you do. You're very clever, but you'll want to focus on what you're doing.

Rat women make great mothers, but Rat fathers are likely to concentrate on bringing home the bacon. Rat men tend to focus on finding someone who will be a great mother to their children and be just as adept in the bedroom and kitchen. However, a Rat man won't expect his wife to work.

You like everything to be in order and in the right place. When you go to other people's houses, even if they are completely spick and span, you'll be able to find something that's not quite right.

If you decide on the career route, then you'll do your best work later in the day. You're great in roles where confidentiality is required, like politics. You're good at keeping secrets. You might 'leak' a little if someone gets you very, very drunk but you'll never give up the good stuff or reveal the whole story – that's for sure.

Rats make great librarians although expect to spend more of your time reading the books than dealing with the customers. You make fantastic solicitors, barristers, actors, singers and anything political; there have been a few Rat Presidents and Prime Ministers. If you're involved in politics of any sort, you will be driven to look after the underdog. Jimmy Carter is a great example of this – he is in his late 90s and is still actively building houses for the poor, alongside his similarly aged wife, Rosalynn. Rosa Parks stood up for black people by refusing to segregate on buses. She took a stand against racism for every black person.

You are great ideas people and often take other people's ideas and turn them into something great. Mark Zuckerberg is an example of this. He is also a standard Rat when it comes to dressing. His style is grey tops and blue jeans. He hasn't got time to think about what he's going to wear so he sticks with what he likes. He's a good example of a Rat – he is who he is and that's how he must be.

On that note you like to look good, but you won't follow fashion trends. You'll find your own style and that can often be quite vintage. You will wear a suit if you absolutely have to but it's not what you want to be in. Cut-off shorts and flip-flops are much more your style. You're very likely to be attractive and often quirky looking.

Love can so very often be about luck so here are some aspects about Rats that you might be able to use in your favour to find your special someone.

You're the sort of person who can take over or carry conversations, so you need to be around strong characters. You can't be in a relationship where you can dominate your partner. They'll need to be able to give as much as they get in the dialogue stakes. Rat women are inclined to choose bad boys for this reason.

On a date you're likely to be in your natural habitat in a pub or pizzeria, even more so if there is a garden area. Concerts are okay but an outdoor concert will suit you down to the ground. You love all of that.

You will always be late, so your date is going to need to expect that. If by some miracle you turn up on time you will arrive completely disorganised. Timekeeping is just not your special skill.

Rats are loyal. When you're in a relationship you will always have your partner's back. However, you will never know when it's time to shut up.

You are up for one-night stands, but ultimately, you're looking for relationships so even dates will be about finding someone you're compatible with long-term.

So, let's get down to business and tell you which signs in the Chinese Horoscopes you should date, love, marry or avoid.

Let's talk about love...

Rat and Rat

If you've checked the chart at the beginning of the book you already know that Rats and Rats make great friends. You will share a mutual love of talking politics, listening to music, and socialising in general, a very strong basis for becoming firm friends.

Your perfect first date is in a wine bar or pub where you can chat to your hearts' content and solve the problems of the world. Music playing in the background is a great addition, yet another shared interest, but make sure you can hear each other speak or it will be frustrating. I'd avoid the cinema or somewhere with loud live music until you know each other much better. Your connection is going to be best made over a chat and a nice glass of something chilled.

If going out for a drink doesn't work for you then think about playing mini golf. It's fun and you'll still get the chance to talk.

THE LOWE DOWN

Rats can marry Rats. A shared love of family and friends connects you both. You are compatible but don't let your capacity to be pals drive you into the friendzone. You'll need to actively reignite the passion every now and then to avoid that.

Verdict: DATE, LOVE, MARRY

Rat and Ox

You'll never have a better BFF than an Ox as a Rat. They are your staunch supporter, and you'll have each other's backs, whatever the challenges. The secrets you tell your Ox BFF will stay between the two of you forever.

You will be the boss in this relationship, and you will be the one setting boundaries for your Ox lover to live within. They will just go with the flow because they are quietly grounded souls.

A walk through the woods enjoying the scent, sounds and peace of nature would suit you both for a first date. After you've filled your boots with the sounds and scents of nature it will be off to a cheeky pub lunch to partake in a little wine and suitable culinary accompaniments.

Street fairs and markets are good for both of you as lovers of being outside. You'll enjoy wandering around the stalls and being in the open air.

THE LOWE DOWN

Yes, Rats and Oxen can get married but it's never going to set the world alight. Just saying... if you're looking for excitement this won't be the match for you.

If you're already in a relationship with an Ox then take the time to inject some excitement, adventure or magic into your lives. You'll get the security you yearn for, but it may get a bit dull.

Verdict: DATE, LOVE, MARRY

Rat and Tiger

Happy days. Tigers are totally compatible with Rats. They love to play just as much. You are both committed to family and friends. If you enjoy being charmed, then the hunter innate in the Tiger will woo you until you give in.

Your perfect first date should involve eating out. You both like your food. Quirky restaurants with dark lighting would work. A bit of adventurous dining like one of the blackout restaurants that have popped up all over the world, where you eat in the dark, would entertain you both. A bike ride for a bit of exercise is another great option.

THE LOWE DOWN

Is this marriage material? Yes, quite possibly. If you let the Tiger take the lead it will end up being a 60%-40% relationship. Guess who has the 60%? You're right – it will be the Tiger.

If you don't mind your Tiger being the boss then this marriage can work, and it will be playful, adventurous and fun.

Verdict: DATE, LOVE, MARRY

Rat and Rabbit

Love, love and more love. This is a match made in heaven. It's such a great combination that you could meet in December and be married by the following July! This is a committed relationship. If you find a Rabbit you've found a partner for life who wants exactly what you want. They will be up for love, romance, marriage, and children.

You'll both try and play it cool as you enjoy each other's company over a great meal but, trust me on this, your Rabbit date will be just as desperate as you to jump in to bed for dessert afterwards.

You could pamper yourselves with a spa date which would work for both of you. This is one of those rare matches where it really won't matter what you do for your first date – you are going to end up in each other's arms whatever you do. Maybe make it special just so you can tell your grandkids about it when the time comes.

THE LOWE DOWN

A huge yes to date, yes to love and yes to marriage.

Verdict: MARRY, MARRY, MARRY

Rat and Dragon

Rats love a bit of intuitiveness in a person and Dragons are one of the most intuitive of the Chinese animals. Invariably they are spiritual types or great leaders, and the two of you will love spending your time putting the world to rights. There will never be a dull moment.

Dragons love the fact Rats are individuals, have a mind of their own and are straight talkers. Not a lot of people tend to stand up to Dragon people.

Your first date could be a rally against nuclear weapons or for action on climate change. You both want to make a difference to the world, and you will work well together on whatever issues and endeavours are important to you. Volunteering at a soup kitchen would appeal to both of you and give you a chance to do something good while getting to know each other.

THE LOWE DOWN

Marriage is a very definite option with your Dragon. It may be a long courtship as your time will be taken up focusing on changing the world.

Verdict: DATE, LOVE, MARRY

Rat and Snake

Snakes are clever. While that's attractive in a person, Rats will find this annoying because you risk being upstaged ("Nobody puts baby in the corner!" as Johnny says from THAT movie). You two aren't a great match. There could be many arguments because you'll really irritate each other.

You are both super competitive so at a stretch your first date could involve a Sudoku quiz given you're both good at figures. So, not very exciting really or step outside your comfort zones with a trip to the local bowling alley!

THE LOWE DOWN

This is all terribly average and ordinary. I would say a definite no to marriage. You could date but it will only ever be one date and that will probably finish early!

Verdict: DATE ONCE, THEN AVOID

Rat and Horse

This is an 'interesting' match. It can work but the odds are that you will clash. The main element for the Horse is fire and yours is water. You like being part of the centre group in some circumstances, but the Horse wants to be the centre of attention – always!

You won't enjoy the Horse wanting to control you and depending on which sort of Rat you are – Fire, Earth, Metal, Water or Wood – you may end up wanting to take all of their clothes and cut them into pieces. Just saying...

Your first date could include drinks and karaoke. You'll both enjoy free-flowing spirits and showing off for an appreciative audience.

An exciting alternative would be to take your Horse flying high in a hot air balloon where your daredevil spirits can be unleashed.

THE LOWE DOWN

So, here's the thing. This CAN be a good match, but it can also go very badly. If I were you, I'd recommend having a fun first date with a lot of drinking and singing. After that I'd keep it as a great memory and move on.

Verdict: AVOID

Rat and Goat

This one is a tough gig. Rats love noise, action and going out. Goats love a bit of quiet, peace and introspection so a touch of each is a good start. A buzzing pizzeria followed by a walk by the sea in the moonlight in peace could really work.

Families are important to Rats and Goats so a date involving family will bring out the best in both of you. You could go out and have your family join you later or even invite your Goat to a family BBQ. This would show how much your family mean to you and that will impress them.

This relationship will be a bit like a pirate ship – a LOT of hard work but the bounty at the end will be worth it.

THE LOWE DOWN

If you're up for the fire and roller coasters of this relationship then my verdict is that marriage is on the cards, with love and happiness in the mix. If not, then you have the capacity to be great friends.

Verdict: DATE, LOVE, MARRY

Rat and Monkey

Well now there is some serious passion in this mix. If you're looking for some hot sex then this will work for you. You complement each other well. You wake up at the same time and enjoy afternoons together. You sure know how to play when the sun sets. Night is your playground.

For your first date my advice is to get a room. Literally! The chances are you will end up in bed so start as you mean to continue. If you can drag yourselves out of the boudoir, then a comedy show would be a brilliant date that you'd both enjoy.

THE LOWE DOWN

This is a complementary mix. You have a lot in common and both enjoy passionate relationships. One warning though: your Monkey may find your constant verbal chatter draining, so keep it in check!

Verdict: DATE, LOVE, MARRY

Rat and Rooster

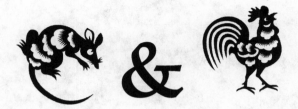

This is not an ideal match. Roosters are morning people, and they are not going to be up for joining you on your late-night adventures. They like and, frankly, need their sleep.

The Rooster will get bored of your views. Roosters don't have particularly strong views on anything. That's not true – they do hate unkindness. They also prefer to walk the walk whereas Rats have a tendency to talk the talk. Roosters want to get down to business and do something about what's important to them.

Date night is fine if you choose an art gallery or museum. Like you, Roosters love history and art so you'll be perfectly in balance for one night, as long as it's not a late one.

An option that would win you a few brownie points would be to take your Rooster to a petting zoo. It would be a unique, thoughtful date your Rooster would appreciate.

THE LOWE DOWN

This really isn't a great match. I wouldn't recommend it. The differences that seem so fascinating when you first meet will drive you crazy in a long-term relationship. Your Rooster will get tired of you talking while they are getting things done, and you'll get fed up with them never joining you for a late-night knees-up.

Verdict: AVOID

Rat and Dog

Dogs are trustworthy, hardworking and methodical. Rats are water element animals, so they tend to prefer to go with the flow.

Dogs love sport whereas Rats are unlikely to have that on their 'to-do' list unless you are watching your children play. While you two can work well together and be friends, it's unlikely you could sustain a long-term interest in each other.

Date night with an excellent pizza and a darn good bottle of something special at your favourite local Italian restaurant would be perfect or swap it for a curry.

Open mic nights would be a great idea as well. A variety of talented souls entertaining you over a pint would be loads of fun.

Rats and Dogs can make a good couple. Dogs can be pessimistic about relationships and love, and Rats can make them feel safe and cared for.

THE LOWE DOWN

There is no question you'll get along with a Dog, but my verdict is that it will not work long term. Friendship is a great option with the trustworthy Dog.

Verdict: DATE, LOVE, MARRY

Rat and Pig

Rats and Pigs have real rapport. You complement each other in every way. You are both intelligent and have many varied views on life. Although Pigs love their solitude Rats are one of the very few Chinese animals who are interesting enough to drag Pigs away from their computers and books.

A perfect date night to take your Pig on would be to a science museum. Follow it up with a glass of excellent wine in a trendy wine bar afterwards to discuss the weird and wonderful things you've seen at the museum.

I can see Rats and Pigs loving a first date on the top level of an open bus tour around the city with the wind in your hair and loving it – learning, chatting and laughing together.

THE LOWE DOWN

My verdict is that there is a lot of potential in this match. If chatty Rats are able to give Pigs some time to indulge their need for solitude you could be a dynamic long-term match.

Verdict: DATE, LOVE, MARRY

THE LOWE DOWN

DATE:

LOVE:

MARRY:

AVOID:

SPECIAL MENTIONS:

Heavenly match

Did you know...?

Rats make great leaders in every form of life – politics, government, civil rights and even in monarchies. Prince Charles, Jimmy Carter, George Bush and Pope Francis are just a few high-profile Rats.

More than a few Rats have had their mouths get them into trouble including Ozzy Osbourne, Elizabeth Holmes and Richard Nixon.

Some Rats have changed the world like Rosa Parks and Alan Turing.

Rats are super individual in their style choices. They are not going to follow the trends in fashion – they have their style and they stick to it – like Mark Zuckerberg, Eminem, Lorde and Katy Perry.

Rats like to be super slim and stylish. RuPaul, Donna Summer, Cameron Diaz, Geri Horner and Trevor Noah are some perfect examples.

Your BFF will more than likely be an Ox, but you'll clash with Horses and drive Monkeys crazy with your incessant chatter.

Ox

The second sign in the Chinese Horoscope is the Ox.

At first sight:

Ox years	You were born after the Chinese New Year in: 1913, 1925, 1937, 1949, 1961, 1973, 1985, 1997, 2009, and if you have just joined us – 2021!
Ox months	Your love mojo is going to be highest in January, May and September. From 6th December and 5th January, you are going to be on fire.
Ox days	Dust off your best dating gear on Wednesdays & Saturdays.
Ox hours	Early bird best hours for you are 9.00-11.00 & 17.00-19.00.
Element	Earth
Top traits	Hardworking, thoughtful, great decision makers & good leaders.

How you're likely to appear on your first date	Very, very casual.
Best colours	You'll rock red, yellow and blue, but ditch the grey it will kill the mood.
Lucky number	Your best number is 9 but 7 just isn't going to work for you.
Lucky direction	Happy days your best directions are Northeast, Southeast & West. Southwest is not the direction you want to be heading.

As an Ox you have some of the valued character traits for a lifelong partnership. You're kind and trustworthy. You are someone people can really count on. You will always help out people you care about. Nothing fazes you – you just get on with it. But you'll only take risks once you've weighed up all of the options. You can be a bit introverted and never like the spotlight on you.

You're an introvert by nature and while you're not opinionated, you don't like injustice and you will make your views clear on that. You're not amongst the more sensitive or intuitive of the Chinese animals. In fact, you have a very thick skin.

You're most at home in a relaxed environment and dressing casually makes you much more comfortable, even though you can pull out the 'fancy' if it's required. You're likely to be found in jeans, sweatshirts, T-shirts or cut-off shorts. You're not inclined to a hippy style; you veer towards the country look.

You can carry a bit of weight in your later life. Oxen are certainly not naturally slim. You love your food – nice hearty meals with steak, chips or dumplings.

You're up for a party but if you're honest you'd prefer a Ploughman's lunch in a pub. You like your alcohol. I've yet to meet an Ox who doesn't like a drink. It chills you out. You try not to be uptight, and you really want people to see you as super relaxed but underneath you often have some tension going on. You go out of your way to help people feel relaxed in your company and you're not one for getting depressed. You'll prefer a smaller group when you're out and about. You can often be a bit of a wallflower in social situations, but once you get to know people, you'll fast become their best mate. You are funny, funny. Anyone going out with you is going to laugh a lot. You have a dry sense of humour. As long as you aren't dashing off somewhere you are kind and thoughtful. But you can be a bit of a moaner.

Food is fuel to you, so you love food from a very practical perspective. You do enjoy wine and beer. Although you'll prefer to eat at home you will go out for a meal, but you're unlikely to spend loads of money on a fancy meal.

You are into everything outdoors, so you'll love staying in a caravan in the woods and walking holidays or dates. It's the simple things like going to the pub and playing darts or snooker or concerts, particularly if they happen to be outside. That doesn't mean you don't like parties – you can really make the magic happen when you throw a party, and everyone will want to come along. You won't be fazed by all of the organising.

It's probably no surprise to anyone, least of all yourself, that Oxen are hard workers. You'll work far more hours than everyone else and won't think anything of it. It's not a conscious thing – it's just what you do. You're not a skiver and working a lot is not hard for you. You want to achieve in your job, and you'll stick it out until the end. You're going nowhere until it's finished.

You've got a strong work ethic just like the animal you represent, and you will tend to be more traditional rather than someone who thinks outside the box. You are by no means a risk taker. However, in areas you know well things will operate really efficiently. You hate failure especially if you've done all of your homework and it's still gone wrong. While you work hard it's just a job to you; home is your castle and strongest interest.

You're efficient and organised. I wouldn't say you are a planner but if you need to get something done you will do the work to make it successful. You're exactly the sort of person people can rely on in a crisis, like a pandemic, as Oxen are survivors. You are dependable but you make everything happen in slow motion.

You do well in jobs in farming, education, and engineering because you are great with your hands. Although law is also an area you would excel in. You would hate doing housecleaning as a job.

Your superpower in your career is that you are happy to work hard, and if your role requires long hours, you will be fine with that. Your weakness is that you will try to please everyone.

Oxen are early risers because you have to be by nature. You want to be lazy but when it comes to work you never are. You're unlikely to ever give yourself 'me time' or time for yourself. You're always on the go and don't know to relax. That said, you can relax when you're with friends and family, and when you go out to eat, but aside from that you just keep going.

You're not going to be into fitness so the gym is definitely not for you, but you're up for anything outdoors, so may be up for walks or treks in the country.

You're not going to be into fast cars. You need to drive something you like but you won't care what age it is. You'll appreciate a 4x4 because it's practical, versatile and can pull a caravan around the countryside. It's not just cars – you're really not materialistic at all. However, you do want what you want so you won't be frivolous when you shop because you know how to look after the pennies. You won't spend money recklessly. You're cautious and read the fine detail.

You like a nice home but if you're left to your own devices your décor will stay the same until a partner decides enough is enough. Your home will look lived in, rather than like a show house. You're not going to feel inclined to change it yourself. Despite being grafters at work at home you're lazy. If people don't come to your place, you will be even lazier. You might be busy outside but inside your home you are not, unless you have no choice, or someone is due to visit. Will you have a pet at home? You'll really appreciate the loyalty of a Dog. It's likely though that you'll appreciate having to be a cat's servant much less.

You love the sun and when you finally stop working so hard you love to go to the country or to an island where you can explore outside, check out the history, with quaint bars to chill out in. If you could retire abroad, you would live your life basking in the sun to warm your ageing bones.

Love can so very often be about luck so here are some aspects about the Ox that you might be able to use in your favour to find your special someone. I wouldn't say Oxen are lucky in love exactly but you'll never give up on your relationship. You'll stick with your partner through thick and thin.

You'll look for love partners with the same values as you, someone who is happy to live a slower pace of life. You'll choose someone who isn't going to bully you to get their own way and you are not going to want a spendthrift. You will be incredibly loyal and faithful once you find your life partner.

You can find yourself living in the past a bit. For this reason, people won't want to cross you because you have a long memory, like an elephant. On the upside you're unlikely to get into arguments, you don't like them, and you'll never be guilty of backbiting. You've always got things to say but you're not going to get super-heated about your opinions. That's one of the reasons you get along so well with Rats. Rats can talk people to death and you're more likely to listen rather than compete for talking time.

You are super compatible with Rats, Monkeys and Roosters.

You like pretty things, and your partners are no different. Chances are you'll have a good-looking type on your arm or to take down the aisle. You could find you're attracted to more extroverted signs, which is so often the way with an Ox. But while you like to be around extroverts you won't want to live with them full-time; you'll prefer to marry an introverted type who prefers a slower pace of life.

You are not going to play games. When you meet that special someone, you are going to do whatever it takes to make your marriage last. You'll put up with negatives and not leave a relationship. You prefer to be in a relationship, even though you don't really need to be around people. You are not a fan of PDAs.

You'll work hard for your partner and children and be trustworthy and do whatever you can for them. You won't mind bringing home the bacon for your loved ones, even if it means working extra hard.

Children are very important to you. You probably left home for a relationship because you don't like living alone. Oxen will put up with things that others won't just to stay in a relationship. For these reasons you're one of the signs who is likely to meet your partner early and stay married forever.

So, let's get down to business and tell you which signs in the Chinese Horoscopes you should date, love, marry or avoid.

Let's talk about love...

Ox and Rat

You'll never have a better BFF than a Rat as an Ox. They are your staunch supporter, and you'll have each other's backs.

If you're in a relationship with a Rat, they will be the dominant partner and they'll be setting the boundaries for you to live within. You'll patiently listen to Rats talk, happy to let them be the extrovert in your partnership.

A walk through the woods enjoying the scent, sounds and peace of nature would suit you both for a first date. After you've filled your boots with the sounds and scents of nature it will be off to a cheeky pub lunch to partake in a little wine and suitable culinary accompaniments.

Street fairs and markets are good for both of you as lovers of being outside. You'll enjoy wandering around the stalls and being in the open air.

THE LOWE DOWN

Yes, Rats and Oxen can get married but it's never going to set the world alight. Just saying... if you're looking for excitement this won't be the match for you.

If you're already in a relationship with an Ox then take the time to inject some excitement, adventure, or magic into your lives. You'll get the security you yearn for, but it may get a bit dull.

Verdict: DATE, LOVE, MARRY

Ox and Ox

On paper this match looks great. You are kind, trustworthy and you can count on each other. You're a hard worker who gets things done. You're both early risers, dress casually, prefer relaxed dates and you're both just easy to get along with.

You'll love a Ploughman's at the pub. Add in some darts or snooker and life will be good. You'll both be up for a bit of music and concerts, especially if they're held outside. Walking holidays and camping will work for both of you.

THE LOWE DOWN

But and this is a but with a capital 'B'. This is just going to be dull. There's no spark. There's no excitement. You can rely on each other but that will work a lot better in a friendship than as lovers.

Friendzone this option quickly. You'll get on great, but this isn't the recipe for a relationship.

Verdict: DATE (THEN FRIENDZONE)

Ox and Tiger

Oxen are home birds. They prefer the simple things in life. You'll love being dressed casually sitting in the pub with a small group of friends. Tigers will not. They are party people. They like different, quirky dates with a bit of excitement.

I suggest a picnic somewhere your Tiger can play on the swings or go for a bike ride. They're unlikely to be happy just 'being as one' with nature as you will be.

THE LOWE DOWN

This match just isn't going to work. I'd recommend avoiding it. Your first date is unlikely to be followed up with a second one.

I wouldn't bother with the first date to be honest.

Verdict: DATE, THEN AVOID

Ox and Rabbit

Oxen and Rabbits are simple folk. They relate to each other in so many areas of life. They both enjoy spending time with family, so a BBQ date with family would work for both.

The important things in life come from your home life; you can expect when you meet each other to share the same values in life.

My recommendations for a first date would be dating with another couple so you can bring your friends along to check out that you have found the one. I suggest pizza for four.

THE LOWE DOWN

This match could go the distance.

Verdict: DATE, LOVE, MARRY

Ox and Dragon

You both love the outdoors so any dates involving walking, picnics, outdoor concerts are going to work for both of you.

You will be more like mates on a first date, but they could end up being a friend for life. I suggest a walk with your Dragon to feed the ducks.

THE LOWE DOWN

You'll enjoy your date together, but this isn't a relationship that's going anywhere really.

Verdict: DATE

Ox and Snake

Dating a Snake is a great idea for an Ox. You have so much in common so pretty much anything you enjoy, they will enjoy as well. You don't even need to come up with date ideas because your Snake is an ideas person so leave them to make the decisions.

Snakes have a huge amount of patience, and the Ox will respect their advice.

With your joint cultured taste, you could stroll around a castle or stately home, followed by a cream tea.

THE LOWE DOWN

Marriage is certainly on the cards for you and your Snake. Go for it. Have loads of laidback dates being entertained by your competitive and attention-seeking Snake and 'put a ring on it'.

Verdict: DATE, LOVE, MARRY

George Clooney is an Ox who lucked out finding his Snake match in the awesome Amal.

Ox and Horse

Horses are full on and like everything to be about them. If you're happy to give them the attention they demand and let them be the boss then you're in for a fun time.

But you're only going to be able to do that for a short time and Horses need it 24/7.

I can only suggest a maze where you could lose each other.

THE LOWE DOWN

They are going to drive you mad. They are far too strong for your gentle ways and the relationship will need to be all their way.

Verdict: AVOID

Ox and Goat

If you're looking for a fiery relationship, then this will be perfect for you. Not in the passionate, rip off each other's clothes sort of a way – in a clashing about EVERYTHING sort of a way.

The Goat is a little more carefree than you could ever face being.

You could try watching a boxing match to watch someone else clashing for a change.

THE LOWE DOWN

Exhausting – give it a miss!

Verdict: AVOID

Ox and Monkey

This match has big possibilities. The laid-back Ox will be brought out of their shell by the cheeky Monkey. Monkeys will bring out the fun streak hidden in the practical, hard-working Ox. The Ox will bring out the home-loving nature in every Monkey.

Although these two animals have such different characteristics, you make up for what is missing in each other. You're both real people who love to share and help each other.

A cookery class for beginners followed by an Italian meal cooked by someone else would be perfect for both of you.

THE LOWE DOWN

I can hear the wedding bells here already.

Verdict: DATE, LOVE, MARRY

Ox and Rooster

This is a great match. Your Rooster will love everything about their hard-working, trustworthy, kind Ox and you will provide solid ground for the trickster Rooster.

Roosters are planners and methodical just like the Ox so you'll both equally love planning for the future and adventures together.

Your Rooster will share the same values in life which means marriage is a definite yes.

Head to a comedy show. It will be laid-back, fun and bring out your shared sense of humour. You'll both love it.

THE LOWE DOWN

You'll make your Rooster so happy that they will crow about their happy marriage to their Ox for decades in your long, happy marriage.

Verdict: DATE, LOVE, MARRY

Ox and Dog

You are both loyal, trustworthy, dependable and kind but there really can be too much of that. Neither of you brings the fun, play or cheekiness both of you need.

Hit the coffee and cake and you'll both love it.

THE LOWE DOWN

Big time friendzone. Nothing to see here.

Verdict: FRIENDZONE

Ox and Pig

You'll be perfect for your Pig. Oxen are such hard workers and your Pig will be as well. The way you love each other is perfectly harmonious but you'll only show your affections behind closed doors.

You both love the outdoors so you could take your Pig horse-riding. It might be a new experience for them so you could splash out on some lessons for your first date. Follow it up with a pub lunch and your Pig will be happy.

THE LOWE DOWN

Send out those invitations for the wedding of the decade.

Verdict: DATE, LOVE, MARRY

THE LOWE DOWN

DATE:

LOVE:

MARRY:

AVOID:

SPECIAL MENTIONS:

Friendzone

Did you know...?

There is no shortage of world leaders and politicians amongst Oxen including Barack Obama, Margaret Thatcher, Hirohito, and Robert F. Kennedy.

Oxen have been high profile world influencers in their area like Malala Yousafzai, Malcolm X and Princess Diana in their own ways.

More than a few Oxen have used their power badly such as Saddam Hussein and Pol Pot.

Oxen more than hold their own amongst the most popular actors of our time – Meryl Streep, Angela Lansbury, Dick Van Dyke, Gal Gadot, Morgan Freeman, Michael J. Fox, Anthony Hopkins, Laurence Fishburne, Jane Fonda, and George Takei. Super sports achievers Mark Spitz, Simone Biles and Naomi Osaka are Oxen. Hard work and persistence clearly pay off in sport.

Oxen prefer people like them or Rats who they can chat with freely. But they're not huge fans of change, so Horses are less likely to work for them.

Tiger

The third sign in the Chinese Horoscope is the Tiger.

At first sight:

Tiger years	You were born after the Chinese New Year in: 1926, 1938, 1950, 1962, 1974, 1986, 1998, 2010 & next year's babies, born after Chinese New Year will be Tigers!
Tiger months	Your best months for love are 5th June to 6th July.
Tiger days	Mondays are your day for love.
Tiger hours	You take night owls to new and interesting levels. Your hottest times of the day are 9pm-11pm.
Element	Wood
Top traits	You are passionate, confident, direct and you mate for life.

How you're likely to appear on your first date	You like dressing up and you will look amazing. You like your clothes and you're not afraid to show off your style.
Best colours	Blues, greens, and browns are awesome for you but avoid red. Purple works as well.
Lucky number	Your best number is 1 but 9 just isn't going to work for you. 1 is water, you are wood and 9 is fire so unless you are looking for some serious heat...
Lucky direction	You want to be heading Northeast and Northwest. East is okay but avoid the West.

You're probably not going to be surprised if I tell you that Tigers are full of themselves. You're very confident in what you do and super outspoken. Nobody could have accused Fidel Castro of pulling his punches when he spoke. You're direct and have been known to say things for effect. You might recognise the late Hugh Hefner in that description. Underneath all of that though is a very gentle person.

You're good at most things because you want to be good at it. Usain Bolt and Richard Branson are both at the top of their game and they are great examples of getting where they wanted to be because of their drive to make it happen. If you're given a schedule to get something done, you will make it happen and be pretty annoyed at anyone who hasn't done their bit. You can be argumentative and can suffer from a bit of depression if you don't get your own way. The flipside of that is that you are passionate in relationships and when you finally meet your partner you mate for life.

Freedom is incredibly important to you. Of all of the Chinese animals the sign least likely to be okay with feeling caged is the Tiger. Best to make sure you don't break the law; prison would be a nightmare for a Tiger.

You're a risk taker, but you feel as though you must fight for what you get. I don't know any Tigers who have had it easy. You work hard and can make a lot of money, but you can often lose it again as is the way of the risk taker.

Tigers are funny and anyone who dates you is going to have a load of fun. You love cinema and chances are you're always deep into binge-watching one boxset or another. TV and movies are big favourites. Jon Stewart is one of the world's most famous Tiger funny men, audiences love his wit.

You love fame and publicity. You can see this in so many of the world's most well-known Tigers – Tom Cruise, Marilyn Monroe, Victoria Beckham and Lady Gaga, who lap up being centre stage.

Shopping is one of your great loves, whether it's clothes, home décor or art. No one who knows you well will be surprised to find you searching out 'just one more piece of art' for your place. You don't just love to look at beautiful, stylish things, you like to be in places where you are regaled with the good things in life. Whether it's the cinema, theatre, art galleries or haute cuisine you like to be entertained.

The gym won't feature in your life unless you've decided you want to lose weight, because you do not find it fun like those gym bunnies in their fancy Lycra. You don't mind outside 'sport' like golf, if you're trying to have some fun and want to lose those extra pounds.

Your favourite time of the year is not summer. Comfortable and cosy clothes are your favourites so the autumn/winter dressing styles are right up your street. You're most likely to be found in jeans, boots, and jumpers. But you really can turn it on when you need to dress up – you can do the black tie, evening dress thing with the best of them and you will look amazing. Clothes are important to you, and you use your style to attract potential love partners. Victoria Beckham is a great example of this. Not only is she super careful about what she wears, she has her own fashion brand. You can see her touch in what she and hubby, David, wear in public.

You love your parents, but you won't be one of those people who keep dossing on their couch. When you leave, you leave. You'll be focused on bringing in the bacon, getting your house sorted and making money. You'll put all your energies into your partner and kids who will be very important in bringing you the happy family life you crave. Once you meet your Mr or Mrs Right, you'll just get married in a whirlwind of romance and passion.

Your house is going to be classic. It could be just like the Gatsby era. It will be flamboyant just like you. You're really into art, décor and furnishings, and your shopping ventures will often be about finding those perfect pieces. For example, if you choose monochrome, the whole house will follow the theme throughout. Your home is your castle.

Holidays are very important to you and if your partner doesn't like them, you'll find yourself a bit bewildered and lost. Holidays are your relaxation time.

In your later years you will love gardening. Your younger years are all about partying. However, whoever does your garden in your earlier years will need to make it beautiful and make sure everything is in its place.

But let's talk about you in love and relationships…

On the dating scene you are a hunter. It won't surprise you to hear that one of the most famous Tigers is Tom Cruise and his hunting ability to find partners is pretty legendary. Marilyn Monroe was another very successful hunter of lovers, and she always got her man. Another famous Tiger lover was Oscar Wilde, and that man had a way with words.

You won't want to hear this, but you are very dominant in relationships. You're reading this now and saying very clearly that you are not! If you were in a row with someone you wouldn't know how to stop it until they have no choice but to admit defeat. My answer to this is to throw water on yourself, but I don't suppose you're going to like that idea. You always want to get your own way and you'll be super touchy if you don't.

You want to mate for life and once you meet 'the one' you won't waste time – you'll marry them swiftly. You will do whatever it takes to keep your family together because family is one of the most important things in your life. You are passionate and fun to be with. Just a reminder though – you really need to ask your partner whether they are into holidays straight up.

You'll move house more than the average person to reach your goal of having your dream home. When your kids leave home, you'll feel like you need to change your home base again with retirement in mind. You're very protective of your children, and just a wee warning – when they are ready to leave home – it's likely you'll feel as though you no longer know what your role is or what you're meant to be doing. This is normal for Tigers. As I said, you'll probably decide on a move and a change of scenery.

Without further ado – let's talk about love…

Tiger and Rat

Happy days. Tigers are totally compatible with Rats. You both love to play just as much. You are both committed to family and friends. Your Rat will enjoy being charmed and the innate hunter in you will woo your Rat until they give in.

Your perfect first date should involve eating out. You both like your food. Quirky restaurants with dark lighting would work.

A bit of adventurous dining like one of the blackout restaurants that have popped up all over the world, where you eat in the dark, would entertain you both. A bike ride for a bit of exercise is another great option.

THE LOWE DOWN

Is this marriage material? Yes, quite possibly. If your Rat lets you take the lead it will end up being a 60%-40% relationship. Guess who has the 60%? You're right – it will be you.

If your Rat doesn't mind you being the boss then this marriage can work, and it will be playful, adventurous and fun.

Verdict: LOVE, DATE, MARRY

Tiger and Ox

Not such great news. This is not a good match. Tigers love to play and are super adventurous. Oxen are home birds. They like a quieter, more laid-back social life.

I can only recommend a picnic with a set of swings for your Tiger to entertain themselves. If your Tiger needs swings to feel entertained while they are with you then… you get the picture!

THE LOWE DOWN

Verdict: AVOID

Tiger and Tiger

Too much of a good thing is the best way to describe this match. Tigers only have two things in common and they are partying and hunting. They'll lead each other on and entice each other into adventures but when the party is over, there's nothing there to build a relationship on.

Have a date by all means, but then give it a miss. Paintballing will work for both combining hunting, playing and adventure, but once the date is done, then go your separate ways.

THE LOWE DOWN

Verdict: DATE, THEN AVOID

Tiger and Rabbit

If passion in your world looks a lot like bickering, then this is a 'passionate' relationship. You have a lot in common which is great for a friendship, but not so great in love partners.

The best I can offer is a date at a cinema, although the chances are that you'll argue over which film to watch...

THE LOWE DOWN

Friendzone your Rabbit pal. You'll spend too much time arguing for this to go anywhere.

Verdict: FRIENDZONE

Tiger and Dragon

Happy days! This is literally a match made in heaven. This relationship has got everything, including the capacity to stay the distance.

It doesn't matter where you take your Dragon on a date, you'll both enjoy whatever the other chooses. If your Dragon wants to go to a book reading, then you'll be up for that. If you want to head to a fun fair, then your Dragon will be in.

THE LOWE DOWN

This match gives me all the wonderful feels.

Verdict: DATE, LOVE

Tiger and Snake

Your Snake will be your perfect partner in crime for fun, partying, and adrenaline. Your Snake will balance out your 'jump in with both feet' in pretty much all situations. They are more conservative and will think through the details you miss.

You'll take the lead, and they will follow. Not much here to form a relationship once you both come back down to earth though.

Enjoy it. Your Snake will definitely be up for paragliding on a date. You'll take the lead, and they'll make sure the safety gear is all in order.

THE LOWE DOWN

Verdict: DATE

Tiger and Horse

Yes! Tiger, your Horse really could be your soulmate. You are both strong characters. You're not going to be dominated by your Horse who is spirited and will join you in your adventures, you're going to be challenged by them. Tigers love a challenge so that will keep your interest.

Your romance is going to be a whirlwind. I suggest a rock concert – you will both love that! You'd both love the adventure and challenge of an Escape Room.

THE LOWE DOWN

Love is in the air!!!

Verdict: DATE, LOVE, MARRY

Tiger and Goat

Your quiet, peace-loving, introspective Goat is not going to be up for partying, and while you can live with a bit of peace and quiet, it isn't your happy place. You will light a fire under your Goat, and they will ground you.

I suggest some fast food and a movie, but your Goat will prefer something less adventurous like *Downton Abbey* whereas you will want *Mission Impossible 4003*. You'll enjoy it but it's not your usual pace and you won't want to do it very often.

THE LOWE DOWN

Depends on your tolerance for quiet. Perhaps just the one date.

Verdict: DATE

Tiger and Monkey

No, no and no. You will not get along with Monkeys. I wouldn't even recommend a date – this is a recipe for a clash. You'll clash in business, and you'll clash in love. Let me give you an example – Monkeys are fun loving and cuddly in relationships whereas a Tiger will feel as though bringing home the bacon is how a person shows love. You are on different wavelengths and there is no middle ground.

I don't recommend a date with a Monkey. Give it a miss!

THE LOWE DOWN

Just... no!

Verdict: AVOID, AVOID, AVOID

Tiger and Rooster

Roosters are a good match for you, Tiger. There is a lot of happy passion in this mix. The trouble will come when you get into a relationship. Both will want to be the boss and there's only room for one. In other matches there may be space for negotiating and compromise, this is not one of those.

A date in a wine bar, with a curry, more wine with a whole lot of flirting.

THE LOWE DOWN

You'll have fun but neither of you will hand over the crown, so marriage is not on the cards.

Verdict: DATE, LOVE

Tiger and Dog

Ah, Tiger, you can go anywhere with your Dog. You have so much in common that any date you like will work for them. There is a lot of mutual respect in this relationship. Where you will jump into a situation without thinking, your level-headed Dog will step in and fix the fallout for you. There is always mutual ground between you.

You are Yin and Yang in the most positive way. Your Dog will be able to talk things through with you in a way other signs won't be able to, and you will listen.

Great dates for you could include sporting events. You would both love being entertained in a corporate box at the cricket with the champagne and great food before and after.

THE LOWE DOWN

Another great match you can make your lifelong partner.

Verdict: DATE, LOVE, MARRY

Tiger and Pig

Hmmm... chances are that you're going to end up in bed wherever you take your Pig. You are always going to be besties, but there's no danger of ending up in the friendzone because there is way too much passion going on between you.

You are a fantastic match in lust and love.

Take your Pig on an intimate evening for two. You get the picture!

THE LOWE DOWN

Hot, hot, hot but a passionate relationship that could end up in marriage.

Verdict: DATE, LOVE, MARRY

THE DOWN LOWE

DATE:

LOVE:

MARRY:

AVOID:

SPECIAL MENTIONS:

Friendzone

Did you know...?

Tigers like keeping active and are into sport so that often keeps illness away but you need to remember to do your warm-up exercises, or you can find yourself with muscle strains.

At first sight Tigers will appear charming, confident, and arrogant and just do first, think later.

Under their cocky surface appearance, Tigers are gentle and committed once they find their lifelong partner, and they are very protective parents.

Tigers are leaders in politics and government. You also tend to like fame and publicity so it's not unusual to find yourself well known in business like Richard Branson, or music like Alanis Morissette, the movies like Jodie Foster or on the telly like David Attenborough or Rosie O'Donnell.

They're winter people so Tigers are into boots, scarves, and jeans but if it's a fancy do expect to be seriously impressed. They brush up VERY well. Think Victoria Beckham and Bradley Cooper.

Tigers are strong authority figures. It suits you. You like to wear crowns in your professional and personal lives. The Queen, Fidel Castro, Narendra Modi, Ayatollah Khomeini, Alexis Tsipras and Kofi Annan are all world leading Tigers.

Tigers gel really well with Pigs, Dragons, Horses, and Dogs.

Tigers are clever, charming, and authoritative but you often jump in and think about the consequences later, and you're not good at getting out of an argument once you're in one.

Tigers clash with Monkeys and Roosters, and they're bored by Rabbits and Oxen. BUT they listen to Dogs.

Rabbit

The fourth sign in the Chinese Horoscope is Rabbit.

At first sight:

Rabbit years	You were born after the Chinese New Year in: 1915, 1927, 1939, 1951, 1963, 1975, 1987, 1999, and 2011.
Rabbit months	Your hottest love months are March, June, and October. Don't go looking for love in September.
Rabbit days	Sunday is your day for love and romance.
Rabbit hours	Your inner party animal comes out to play from 7pm to 11pm.
Element	Wood
Top traits	You are blessed with a kind, forgiving and generous nature.

How you're likely to appear on your first date	On a blind date you'll be in your black trousers with a top with a splash of sassy... probably red.
Best colours	You'll look hot in black, red, blue, and pink. Avoid yellow it will put out your spark.
Lucky number	1, 4 and 9 work for you. 5 is not so great.
Lucky direction	North is literally your 'true north' for love and career. Northwest will bring helpful people into your life. East will bring a bit of romance. West will bring arguments and disagreements.

Great news! Rabbits are SO lucky in love. Everyone will fall in love with you so you're always going to be spoiled for choice.

But before we get into your best matches, let's talk some more about you.

Rabbits are so kind. You will do anything for anyone. You're the type to buy dinner for a homeless person. Your generosity is boundless. More than that – you're quick to forgive. Rabbits are great friends to have on your side. Picture yourself as one half of Thelma and Louise and you'll get the picture. The flipside to that lovely nature of yours is that you can be sensitive and emotional. This can be to your detriment – you can take things too much to heart because you are so kind.

Family is so important to you, and you invest time and energy in those relationships. You love kids and are very likely to have one but stop there and then borrow friends' and relatives' kids. Kids will love spending time with you as well.

You're a party animal but on the flipside you really need and enjoy time on your own. There is a very distinct extrovert and introvert in you Rabbits, a great yin/yang balance.

At school you would've been studious – a total swot. But when you escape, you're likely to be a rule breaker. You want 'to break free'. You're a hard worker and tend to work in spurts, then you're inclined to just take a random day off and spend it walking on a beach. You'll have a career and you'll be great at it, whatever you choose to do. You are just as good at your time off, so you'll be one of the signs most likely to achieve a healthy balance between the two.

You will be suited to anything to do with working with people. Your superpower is the easy way you connect with people. People are infatuated with Rabbits; they love you guys! Human resources, lawyers, recruiters, and counsellors are just some of the many career options.

Your weaknesses at work or in business are that the very generous part of you will say yes to everything and then run out of time. That will stress you out and make you feel completely overwhelmed, and less than surprisingly that can make you ill.

In your free time being outside is going to be your first choice. That said, you'll love your time at home as well. And when winter kicks in you'll choose cosy time indoors at night over outdoor activities.

You won't want to get fat so you will go to the gym or exercise, but only in short bursts and only until you've kicked those few pounds you don't want to keep around. You're no gym bunny, you'll only ever find yourself there if you've overindulged and want to kick the wee tyre around your belly.

You love food and wine and going out for meals. Glamming it up and heading out for meals will be right up your street. Food festivals are on your radar. Your vices are many and varied. Gin and tonic, Haribos, cheeses, sparkly treasures from bags to sunglasses and everything in between. You'll want the best of what you have, so if you are into sporty outfits then they'll need to be the very best, and preferably with a top brand label.

Your home reflects your fantastic yin/yang balance. When you're going out on a date every piece of clothing even vaguely likely to be considered will have been pulled out and those you don't wear will be left lying around your room. Then the next day or the day after you'll run around picking it all up and putting it away. You're both messy and tidy. Your kitchen will show this contradiction. You will have loads on the counters. You want to be tidy and lean towards it but fall at the last hurdle at keeping it tidy all of the time. If you've got people coming around though they'll never know about the untidy moments. Your home will be classy, but it will be a place people feel they can relax. Your sofa will be uber-comfortable with soft, comfy teddy bear throws to snuggle down with.

You do like your brands and labels, but your shopping adventures are also very likely to include shops with unusual and quirky mirrors and paintings. Your cars are going to be sporty little numbers and even when you have children and need more practical options, they'll be branded options like BMW, Range Rover or Audi.

You have a wardrobe for every occasion. You probably have one for jumping out of a plane or snorkelling. You are very fashion conscious and tend to follow the trends.

You can be opinionated but you're unlikely to spend much time pushing it on anyone. Chances are you'll get distracted by something and go off on a tangent. You can be a little bit like a butterfly in that regard.

Rabbits have strong intuitive abilities. Whether you choose to use or develop these abilities or not can come down to your upbringing and family. If your parents struggled to understand your skills, then you've probably kept them quiet until you found someone who is okay with them.

So, what about love and relationships?

Rabbits prefer to be in a relationship. While you like time by yourself you'll always choose being in a twosome over being single. When you make the decision to get married, you'll be in it for life. However, if your partner becomes too demanding or doesn't pay you enough attention then divorce will be a definite option. Family is very important to you and you're a generous and kind soul, but everyone has their limits. You will be up for kids, but even if you only have one, there will always be kids around you.

You need someone who stretches you, who won't let you get away with being too controlling. You want someone who adores you and makes you feel secure in their love. You will love them and give them your full attention, and you'll expect that back in return. You family is so important to you that your lover will need to get on with them.

In love you need to find someone who really cares about you and your pets. They'll need to love children and be comfortable being surrounded by them. An explorer who loves to party will tick a couple of important boxes. You want them to be up for quiet nights in with a chilli but also join you for cocktails and meals out. If they love history and long walks you are on a winner.

Your favourite dates are going to include bars, restaurants, parties, concerts, food festivals, exploring historical buildings and quiet nights in front of the TV snuggled under a teddy bear throw on a comfy couch watching suspense-filled action thrillers.

Your lucky dates can expect you to dress to impress, be engaging and keep them in fits of giggles. You'll have loads to chat about. If you fall in love, they'll get someone who knows how to love well. They can expect a very organised love interest. But if they start playing games with you or are unfaithful, you'll be out the door and not look back. You are loyal and faithful until you are let down. That's not to say you won't have one-night stands or casual relationships, but once you settle down, you're a one-person Rabbit.

You might struggle in a relationship with an early bird because you are very much a night owl.

So, let's get down to business and tell you which signs in the Chinese Horoscopes you should date, love, marry or avoid.

Let's talk about love...

Rabbit and Rat

Wow – love, love, and more love. This is a great combination. You could meet in December and be married by the following July.

This will be a committed relationship. You have found someone who wants exactly what you want – love, romance, and children.

It doesn't matter what date you go on; you will end up in each other's arms whatever date you take your Rat on.

THE LOWE DOWN

Rabbits can marry Rats.

Verdict: DATE, LOVE, MARRY

Rabbit and Ox

You'll have a nice date together, but this isn't going anywhere. There's no real spark in this relationship. Both of you want different things out of life. The Ox is not a risk taker whereas you are, and you'll get frustrated by the Ox's dithering.

Your best options for dates would be a double date with your proper animal matches. I can't even suggest a date option here.

THE LOWE DOWN

Verdict: DATE

Rabbit and Tiger

You have so much in common, but your families will get in the way. That's not the worst of it – you will spend a LOT of time bickering. The Rabbit wants more passion, and the Tiger wants more action.

I'm recommending a date at the cinema but be warned you'll argue about which movie to watch and whether to get popcorn or not. Still at least watching a movie will give you less time to argue.

THE LOWE DOWN

A lot of bickering and none of the good sort of passion.

Verdict: AVOID

Perhaps Johnny Depp (Rabbit) and Amber Heard (Tiger) should have read this book before they got married.

Rabbit and Rabbit

You and your Rabbit will have great dates. You have loads in common. You love and hate all of the same things.

Whatever date you would choose for yourself will work for your Rabbit. You could go to the races for the day, or an amazing gastro pub meal or on a hot air balloon ride.

You could marry your Rabbit, but it could get very mundane if you don't keep the spice up in your relationship.

THE LOWE DOWN

Verdict: DATE, LOVE, MARRY

Rabbit and Dragon

Your Dragon will respect you but will find your slow pace of life a bit boring. You love to play but not as much as your Dragon, so you'll find definite differences in your lifestyles.

This is a friendzone option. You'll make great friends, but you won't ever be more than that.

A fun date you'd both enjoy would be a festival filled with lots of distractions.

THE LOWE DOWN

Friendship for this one.

Verdict: FRIENDZONE

Rabbit and Snake

Wow this is NOT for you. You are going to be completely overwhelmed by your Snake date and not in a good way. They are totally OCD on the tidiness front, and you are so much more relaxed about all that stuff.

You eventually tidy up your house, but you don't get all stressed about it. Do NOT date at their house or yours or you won't make it past the starters.

I can only recommend a quick coffee and then wave each other goodbye.

THE LOWE DOWN

This isn't even something that will turn into friendship. You'll make each other really uncomfortable.

Verdict: AVOID

Rabbit and Horse

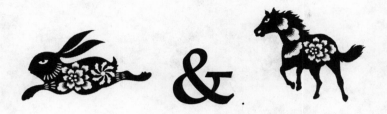

Rabbits and Horses both love to talk… but don't necessary listen to each other! The Horse will have so much energy and while you will try to keep up you will eventually get bored of trailing behind the Horse.

This is a great friendship, but it won't really make the grade as any sort of relationship.

Date somewhere in public where the Horse can be seen, and the Rabbit can watch others while it listens to the Horse chattering on.

THE LOWE DOWN

Definite friendzone.

Verdict: FRIENDZONE

Rabbit and Goat

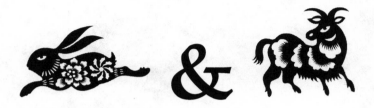

Ooh, you two could get married because you both have easy-going natures and both fully appreciate life.

You are both born to nurture, and if you go on to have children, they will be sure to be brought up in a loving environment.

Your perfect date would be a romantic movie so you can snuggle up together.

THE LOWE DOWN

Verdict: DATE, LOVE, MARRY

Rabbit and Monkey

Although you both have different personalities you share a great sense of humour. There will be a lot of laughter and fun in a shared life with your Monkey. You complement each other with you being the outgoing one and your Monkey taking the role of problem solver.

A comedy show would suit you both. I can see a lot of laughing and looking into each other's eyes. You will be creating your own romantic movie.

THE LOWE DOWN

Laughter is what gets relationships through the tough times so this match has legs.

Verdict: DATE, LOVE, MARRY

Rabbit and Rooster

This match should be spelled C-L-A-S-H. Under no circumstances can I see this working out. But you may end up lifelong friends as you actually have similarities: you love the same music, food, art… it's endless.

A date on an open-top bus, dressed appropriately for the weather, but you will already have this covered.

THE LOWE DOWN

Don't go there!

Verdict: FRIENDZONE

Rabbit and Dog

This can really work because both of you like to do your own thing and you recognise that in each other. Both of you are loyal and trusting animals, so you will relax into each other's company and feel safe and secure.

Go somewhere you can talk on your first date, because you will do a lot of that. Restaurants, cafés, and wine bars are a great option as long as you don't have to shout to hear each other.

A walk around a lake to feed the ducks holding hands and chatting.

THE LOWE DOWN

You can marry your Dog.

Verdict: DATE, LOVE, MARRY

Rabbit and Pig

This is great match, which could very well go the distance. You are both considerate people, and the relationship will be easy-going.

Your Pig will support you and you will return the favour with lots of affection.

You can invest in a great date with your Pig. Maybe a weekend abroad. If there is sea, wine, and you both have your phones you will be happy.

THE LOWE DOWN

This a good match. I can see you two together for the long haul.

Verdict: DATE, LOVE, MARRY

THE DOWN LOWE

DATE:

LOVE:

MARRY:

AVOID:

SPECIAL MENTIONS:

Friendzone

Did you know...?

One Rabbit known for his kindness and sensitivity was Robin Williams.

Rabbits love their fashion and brand labels – think David Beckham, Vidal Sassoon, Hubert de Givenchy, and Ralph Lauren.

Some famous Rabbits that people were well and truly charmed by were Cary Grant and Frank Sinatra.

Rabbits can be super funny – think Mike Myers, Lisa Kudrow, Johnny Galecki, and the late, great Robin Williams.

There are some great influencers in politics and literature amongst Rabbits – Margaret Atwood, George Orwell, Seamus Heaney and, perhaps, more directly Michelle Obama and Gordon Brown.

Dragon

Dragon is the fifth Chinese Horoscope sign.

At first sight:

Dragon years	You were born after the Chinese New Year in: 1928, 1940, 1952, 1964, 1976, 1988, 2000 and 2012.
Dragon months	You'll be firing on all your love cylinders in December, August and September. From 5th April to 5th May, you are going to be on fire!
Dragon days	Dust off your best dating gear on Fridays.
Dragon hours	You're an early riser, usually between 7am and 9am. Your favoured hours are between 5pm and 7pm.
Element	Earth

Top traits	You are highly spiritual souls and people are going to want to be around you all of the time. You enhance their lives just by being in it.
How you're likely to appear on your first date	You're on trend. Matching colours work for you. Dragon women are known for being a little sexy and the men are suave.
Best colours	You'll rock red, yellow, white and blues. Green will be a total mood killer.
Lucky number	4 is your lucky number but 3 is not going to do you any favours.
Lucky direction	Your best directions are Southwest, West, and Southeast. But you do not want to be heading Northwest.

Let's talk about you...

You Dragons are totally out there. There's a reason that there are Dragons leading every Chinese New Year celebration. You are mesmerising and can hold a room when you're talking about subjects you're passionate about.

You live a very full life. You're ambitious and work hard to get where you want to be. You brim with enthusiasm and that will bring you financial gain, even if you're in a support role like a partner.

You are doers and achievers. You're confident and charming. You're a very definite extrovert and the leader of the pack. You're super-opinionated and give great advice.

You are studious, excellent students with a thirst for knowledge. You are a champion for the underdog always and you'll react to witnessing bullying, injustice, or unfairness. That sensitivity to others can make you a touch oversensitive. Alongside that you are super intuitive.

You really like your food, but not takeaways or fast food. You love travel and being introduced to foods and recipes from around the world really floats your boat. You love cooking for family, but you're less inclined to cater for a big gathering.

You love a party, and you will hold your own with the dancing and socialising. That's why you get along with Roosters so much because they love it too. You'll always love your partying and wine but as you get older your tastes will become more refined and slightly slower paced. But you are very yin/yang when it comes to partying – you are well up for a celebration of any type, but you must have alone time to read and re-energise. You are very, very definitely a night owl when you're younger, but after you hit your 60s, if you're not out and about, you'll be in bed by 10pm.

PDAs are common with you – whether you're sharing them with friends, family or lovers.

But you can make mistakes because you're so busy trying to juggle too many balls. You can overlook the little things and that can get you into trouble. Your weakness is that you can trust the wrong people and that can stop you in your tracks.

Gym bunny you are not. Your exercise is more likely to be walking or running because you are outdoor types. You might try the gym out, but you'd rather have what you need at home and use YouTube to get your sessions in. Tai Chi or some sort of other physical activity like that will really work for you. You'll look after your weight, and if you find yourself putting it on, you'll notice and take measures to get rid of it again.

Careers that work for you are going to be about doing what you enjoy. But getting stuck in an office all day is not going to suit you at all. Routine is not something you're comfortable with, but you will have jobs where you can lead. Journalism, health industry, teaching or politics are all jobs that will really suit you. You must find yourself inspired by what you're doing, or you won't stick around.

Your superpowers in your work, business or career are your incredible intuition and your capacity to charm all the people, all of the time.

Home is really important to you. It's going to have a very homely feel. If you have the money your furniture will be beautiful, but regardless of your budget it will always look and feel loved and lived in. That's not to say it won't be stylish – it will, and it will have a consistent theme throughout. You're not exactly minimalist but you won't have a lot of clutter. You won't have stuff around you that doesn't make you happy.

If you can afford the car you dream of you will get it but it's going to need to have a practical element. You will go for something stylish and it's likely to have a soft top.

Fashion-wise you're very clear about what you like. Brands are less important, but you will always dress appropriately, and whatever you wear will get noticed. You'll be just as comfortable in jeans, tops, and jumpers during the day and for relaxed dates as you will be with the sparkle for nights out and special celebrations.

You will want children and you'll be an excellent parent.

Let's talk about love, baby…

When you're looking for a love partner, trust and intelligence are top of the list. You're spiritual and a great talker and those characteristics in your special someone will really work for you. Find someone who loves music, socialising, and family, and you are on a winner.

Your ideal dates would be mingling at social occasions. A nature walk with a cosy lunch in a country pub would be your thing. You'll love dinner parties with friends. Exploring historical buildings and family get-togethers will also float your boat.

Dragons ultimately want a partner. Single Dragons are very sad. There are two types of Dragons – some of you will be up for one-night stands, especially in your younger years, but there's another type who really will not.

When you find the right partner, you will marry for life. Even if your relationship gets stale or breaks up you will look for another long-term relationship. You're very likely to commit and marry early to your partner when you've found the right one. You're loyal and love deeply and need that in return.

You'll respect your lover's careers and their work choices but you're very happy when they're at home sharing your home.

So, let's get down to business and tell you which signs in the Chinese Horoscopes you should date, love, marry or avoid.

Let's talk about love...

Dragon and Rat

Dragons are one of the most intuitive of the Chinese animal signs and Rats love a bit of intuitiveness. You are spiritual, great leaders and you can spend a lot of your time putting the world to rights. There will never be a dull moment.

You will love that your Rat is an individual and has a mind of their own. They will tell you what they think and not a lot of people will stand up to you.

Your date will be a rally against nuclear arms or for climate change. You both want to make a difference to the world, and you'll work together on that.

THE LOWE DOWN

This relationship has the potential for marriage. However, it may be a long engagement as each of you gets side-tracked changing the world.

Verdict: DATE, LOVE, MARRY

Dragon and Ox

This match is never going to set the world on fire and won't get past dating.

I would suggest a date feeding the ducks. It's outdoors and you will both enjoy that.

You both have different and complementary strengths in life, but you won't give each other the time or space to work that out.

THE LOWE DOWN

This is never going to take off.

Verdict: DATE

Dragon and Tiger

This is an awesome match, if a little volatile. You are going to really love spending time together and making plans for your future. You're both full of ideas and your passion for travel could literally take you anywhere.

To be honest, you could go anywhere on your date and you'll love it. My suggestions are a winter wonderland. For a longer date the Orient Express to Paris will work for both of you, big time.

THE LOWE DOWN

You could definitely end up marrying your Tiger.

Verdict: DATE, LOVE, MARRY

Dragon and Rabbit

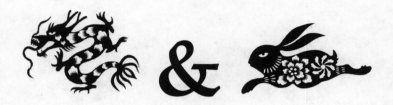

There really is nothing to see here. This match isn't going to make it out of the friendzone. You admire each other's abilities, but you have such different temperaments. You're both strong individuals but you will try and control your Rabbit, and this will clash with a Rabbit's need for freedom.

If you're going to give one date a go I'd recommend a festival – somewhere with lots of distractions to keep you both entertained.

THE LOWE DOWN

This one will friendzone itself fairly quickly.

Verdict: FRIENDZONE

Dragon and Dragon

This is a seriously sexy match. You both have a lot in common and your connection will be pure fire.

Wear red and black on this date... Yep, I do mean your underwear as well. Your date should take advantage of your shared naughtiness.

Perhaps take your Dragon to a late-night club. It's going to be a long, sexy night followed by breakfast as dessert.

THE LOWE DOWN

Too much fire doesn't bode well for a long-term relationship, but your dates are going to be memorable.

Verdict: DATE

Dragon and Snake

This match is worth the extra effort. You are going to be a great and romantic match.

Go straight for the top shelf date for this one. Splash out on a flight to New York with plenty of champagne on the way. Trust me, it will be worth the investment.

THE LOWE DOWN

This is a hot match and has the capacity to go the distance. Go for it!

Verdict: DATE, LOVE, MARRY

Dragon and Horse

You two are going to end up in the friendzone, but let your Horse pick your date. It will be wild and wacky, that's for sure. There will be no shortage of passion in this match, but your Horse will want to control you and there's no chance any Dragon is going to accept that.

I'm guessing something like banger racing, with both of you in cars set for scrapping and racing each other over dirt tracks. It will be great fun.

THE LOWE DOWN

It's not going to go the distance, but your date will be different and fun.

Verdict: DATE, FRIENDZONE

Dragon and Goat

This match is going to be a giant YAWN. No spark, no passion, no real interest.

No date has the power to resurrect something that never gets off the ground. Maybe a quick cuppa and piece of cake somewhere just to be polite?

THE LOWE DOWN

No, no and no.

Verdict: AVOID

Dragon and Monkey

This is a weird one that could go either way. You could find yourself in the friendzone or married. There are not too many matches with the potential to end up either way, but this is one of them.

You'll bring the kid out in each other so a great date would be to walk along the pier, have a go at the fruit machines and buy each other candy floss and ice cream.

Whatever way the relationship goes, the date will be fun.

THE LOWE DOWN

This can go either way – you could be married and stay together forever or find yourselves squarely in the friendzone. Whatever you decide – your dates will be great fun.

Verdict: FRIENDZONE OR DATE, LOVE, MARRY

Dragon and Rooster

You two need what the other has. You are bound to be great friends. Your Rooster will appreciate the knowledge you have and will want to hear all about it. You need your Rooster for their ability to have fun.

Roosters can be wild, and life can get a bit serious for Dragons with their need to contribute to the world, so they will bring you out of that seriousness for a bit.

An option that would win you a few brownie points would be to take your Rooster to an all-night party or hire a couple of motorbikes for the day. Another great option would be to take them to a MotoGP race.

Remember that your Rooster likes their sleep and is usually an early riser, so not too many all-night parties.

THE LOWE DOWN

Marriage is a very definite possibility with this match.

Verdict: DATE, LOVE, MARRY

Dragon and Dog

This one is complicated. Initially I would say avoid because you two will love a good argument, but often people who end up rowing enjoy the making up bit as well. It really could go either way.

I would recommend somewhere outside like a market where one of you can walk off in a huff without entertaining a captive audience, which would be the case in a restaurant.

THE LOWE DOWN

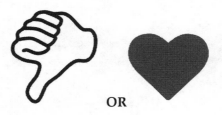

OR

Wow this one is a tough one. Anything from avoid right through to marry. It really depends on how much you enjoy arguing and making up.

Verdict: AVOID OR DATE, LOVE, MARRY

Dragon and Pig

The thing that links you two is your shared intelligence. You'll love to debate and share the latest news of the day. You will stimulate each other mentally.

If the relationship moves into more intimate catch-ups, then you'd better be up to date with the latest sex moves.

A date to a book launch with a fancy bottle of wine afterwards would work for you both.

THE LOWE DOWN

Go for that date, but you're most likely going to end up friends in the long-term.

Verdict: DATE, FRIENDZONE

THE LOWE DOWN

DATE:

LOVE:

MARRY:

AVOID:

SPECIAL MENTIONS:

Friendzone

Did you know...?

A lot of Dragons have been heads of government including Kamala Harris, François Mitterrand, Vladimir Putin, Imran Khan, Boris Johnson and Hosni Mubarak.

Dragons want to change the world and some who have in their fields are John Lennon, Chadwick Boseman, Maya Angelou, Emma Stone, and Melinda Gates.

High-profile Dragons who have fought for civil and human rights include Martin Luther King, Joan of Arc, Che Guevara and Noam Chomsky.

Dragons can be super stylish and some of those who have influenced the fashion world are Christian Dior, Elle Macpherson, Raquel Welch and Isabella Rossellini.

Dragons are great thinkers and in their ranks are people like Charles Darwin and Sigmund Freud.

Snake

Snakes are the sixth sign in the Chinese zodiac.

At first sight:

Snake years	You were born after the Chinese New Year in: 1929, 1941, 1953, 1965, 1977, 1989, 2001 or 2013.
Snake months	You are going to be at your hottest in January, April, May, August & September giving you loads of time to fall in love.
Snake days	Monday is your best day for everything, especially dating.
Snake hours	If you roll out of bed any earlier than 7am you can be a bit grouchy. Although you can dance all night you prefer an early night. Try to be in bed by 21.00 when you are tired especially because this can be a clash hour for you.

Element	Fire
Top traits	You're intelligent, intuitive, and always on time.
How you're likely to appear on your first date	Wherever you are you'll dress to impress. Whether it's for work or dating you'll always be noticed.
Best colours	You'll shine in blue, red and pink. You'll look fab in the sparkly stuff as well but avoid dull colours.
Lucky number	Your best numbers are 4 and 9, 1 isn't the number for you.
Lucky direction	Happy days you can head Northeast & Southeast & West. Northwest is not the direction you want to head in.

Let's talk about you!

Snakes have some of the same strong characteristics as real-life Snakes. You're silent and patient, watching all of the time, getting ready for when you need or want to pounce. People should never underestimate you. Your thoughts run deep and you're a planner. You plan everything before you take action. You're no risk taker.

Patience is a real strength of yours. You plan right down to the exact moment to implement your decisions, whether it's about family or business. Nothing gets past you without being thoroughly investigated. Added to that you are very intuitive. You hone your intuition from a very young age and you're generally right.

You might have found that you were overlooked within your family, especially if there were a lot of you, and had a tendency to be shy. If you choose to have kids, you'll be an awesome parent. You'll be really in touch with their feelings. It's so important to you that you will want to be seen as a super parent.

Others will see you as an extrovert because that's how you appear, however, you are very much an introvert at heart. While you have opinions you only choose to share them with people you know really well, otherwise you will stay quiet.

You were great at school. You were studious and would've been horrified if you'd found yourself in detention. You would've worked much harder than everyone else to get to the top of your class.

Snakes are the most sensitive of all of the Chinese animals; you're closely followed by Dragons. You will be able to answer most people's questions before they finish asking them.

You love your food. Chances are you'll have a taste for a certain type of alcohol. You might love your wine but you're just as likely to stick to Tia Maria. You like going out for dinner as part of a couple or small group. You're less likely to enjoy large parties. Crowds are not your thing. You love being at home and time on your own to wind down.

Music and gossip are your thing, and you may have dabbled with some of the softer drugs in your teens, but it really isn't your scene. You are up for boozy nights with your friends but you're unlikely to be found indulging in any vices seriously or on your own.

You're no gym bunny but if you feel like you are putting on weight then you will often go to the extreme on weight loss programs to get rid of the excess fat. Cakes and sweets would be on the blacklist until you were happy with your size again. Being slim is important to you and you'll hit the gym and do the exercise to make that happen.

Snakes are outdoor types and homebodies equally. You love to be in the sun. The rain is not for you though. On dark nights you'd much rather be snuggled up on the sofa with your partner than out and about.

There are two types of Snakes when it comes to careers. One is all about your career with everything else a firm second. However, there is another type who will have a job, but their family is their top priority. Which one are you?

You're great with figures and shrewd and astute. If your job involved purchasing and investments, then you are perfect. Snakes love money and are both savers and spenders. So, if you can see a chance to make money then you will be an excellent entrepreneur. You are super creative and can think outside the box in most situations. Think accountants, claim assessors, librarians, or forensics bods. Your superpower is that you carefully plan your investments. Your weakness? You're prone to a bit of self-indulgence.

Don't even think about doing anything mundane. It will do your head in. Working in a factory where you can't use your brain won't work for you, and you're not one for physical jobs.

Your home is never going to be cluttered. If it's small, then it might appear like that but you're not a hoarder and you never will be. In a larger house you will have ornaments and loads of photos of family and friends. It will look like a mini gallery. You have unusual taste which will be super stylish and eye-catching. You'll be the house with the unusual clock or painting.

In fashion terms you're more likely to choose comfy styles during the day but you really know how to dress up for every type of occasion. You are into fancy brands and cars. If you have the money, then everything you own will be just like that. If you don't then you will be super astute at finding sites where you can get them at bargain prices.

Are you ready to talk about love?

In love you're looking for intelligent people who know how to work hard. When you're lucky enough to find that then you're married for life. You're one of the animal signs that believes that if there are problems in a relationship, they can be worked out. If you hit a rough patch, then you will have the patience to put your love life back on track.

You will always prefer to be in a relationship. Snakes are not happy being by themselves all of the time, not least because they love to chat.

Chances are that you'll search out career types who can bring home money when you're ready to date. You love money and you save and spend, but money is a priority in your life. You're looking for kindness, intelligence, and a great conversationalist. Family will need to be important to your love interest. You want, and need, someone who will love you just as you are.

The dates that will work for you are concerts, theatre and you'll prefer going out as a couple or family, especially over a meal. Going on holidays as a family is one of your favourite things. You can rest and relax knowing that everyone around you is happy and having fun.

Your date can expect someone really flirty. Once you get past the first 15 minutes of knowing someone, you'll be chatty. As long as you've planned every bit of your date then you'll be happy with whatever the date is. You do not like surprises. You can a teeny bit (or a LOT) OCD when it comes to planning dates. You love a cuddle, but the chances are that that isn't going to happen until the two of you are alone.

You are up for one-night stands but not if you're in a relationship, and as long as you retain the attention of your partner then you will stay faithful for life.

You'll be up at 7am, but not fit for human contact before that. You'll work hard and be proactive during the day, but you'll get tired by 9pm and usually go off to bed. If you're going out though you can stay awake with everyone else.

Kids and grandkids are important to you. You'll love playing with them and teaching them stuff. You'll be the parent or grandparent who will be sitting on the floor being silly with them.

Let's take a look at your best romantic matches.

So, let's get down to business and tell you which signs in the Chinese Horoscopes you should date, love, marry or avoid.

Let's talk about love...

Snake and Rat

This isn't a great match to be honest. Rats are water elements which means you will clash, and the rest of the time won't be anything to write home about either. It's all just a bit ordinary.

You are going to be too bombastic for a Rat and... well... there's just not going to be any spark. Why? What happens when fire (you) meets water (them) – they put your fire, passion and spark out!

My only suggestion is somewhere outdoors where you don't have to talk, which rather defeats the purpose of a date. Perhaps a petting zoo?

THE LOWE DOWN

Date if you must but I wouldn't put you together by choice. Do NOT marry.

Verdict: DATE

Snake and Ox

Snakes & Oxen have so much in common they will enjoy their time together whatever they do.

You may take the lead and plan the date, but you can be assured your Ox will be pleased with your choice.

When you know each other better you'll plan all of your dates to make sure both of you are happy. You'll have a very harmonious relationship.

So many dates will work but some of my suggestions for you to spoil your Ox are an outdoor date at a fete or sightseeing, followed by a delicious cup of hot chocolate or a freshly squeezed juice, depending on the weather.

THE LOWE DOWN

You can marry your Ox.

Verdict: DATE, LOVE, MARRY

Snake and Tiger

You tend to prefer a quieter life… until you meet your Tiger.

This is a daredevil match made in heaven. You are both going to want to push the boundaries big time and you'll have great fun doing it. Paragliding, abseiling, skydiving, a balloon ride – any of these will make both of you adrenaline junkies happy. You'll love it equally.

But sadly, when the dust settles life is not always about adrenaline kicks…

THE LOWE DOWN

Once the adrenaline has died down there's not much left to base a match on. Tigers are party animals and while you don't mind going out, you're just as happy snuggling up at home.

Verdict: DATE

Snake and Rabbit

Oh, dear this is not a great match. Your Rabbit will be totally overwhelmed by you and your tendency to be bombastic. Rabbits are a wee bit messy, although they do eventually get around to tidying up.

Whereas you are OCD about tidiness. It will drive you crazy.

No dates at each other's houses or this will be a very short acquaintance. My suggestion for a date is to go to a book reading.

THE LOWE DOWN

This one just isn't going to work. Have a date, not at either of your homes, and leave it as a pleasant memory.

Verdict: DATE

Snake and Dragon

This could be a match made in heaven. You can be BFFs and lifelong love partners. I would pull out all of the stops for this one.

Take your Dragon on a day trip to Paris, with lunch overlooking the Seine and many or several glasses of the finest champagne. This match is worth it.

THE LOWE DOWN

Yes, you two could go the distance.

Verdict: DATE, LOVE, MARRY

Snake and Snake

This is a match made in hell. If you want to spend your time scoring points at each other's expense and arguing about EVERYTHING then marry another Snake. This is not going to work.

I can't even recommend a date here. You will both want to organise it and you'll both get all OCD about it. Smile, wish them well and walk away... FAST!

THE LOWE DOWN

Nope, this is not going to work.

Verdict: AVOID

Snake and Horse

You both love figures and being terribly clever at it: I can see you both on your tenth Sudoku puzzle book and bragging about it. You'll enjoy making each other look good and feeling mega intelligent.

You are a quiz team dream so that's an option. But I think you and your Horse would love an Escape Room or murder mystery night and you'd both shine. And you'll probably win.

THE LOWE DOWN

You make great friends and will really enjoy each other's company but there's unlikely to be much romance in this.

Verdict: DATE, BUT REALLY FRIENDS

Snake and Goat

Both of you are uber-creative and highly intelligent. Your Goat will appreciate your intellect and you'll admire their negotiating powers. There is a lot of mutual respect going on here.

But that's as far as it goes for you two. There are no sparks at all. I can't even see you really being friends to be honest.

The only date I can suggest is somewhere really noisy where you can ignore each other at opposite ends of the room.

THE LOWE DOWN

I'd give this one a miss.

Verdict: AVOID

Snake and Monkey

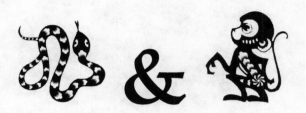

This match has potential. You can be BFFs, but there's very clear chance for marriage in this mix. You get along on most things. Except politics – avoid politics. You are literally fascinated and intrigued by each other.

There is a danger though that it will slip into the friendzone and there will be no passion. Beware of that.

Any date that involves coffee and cake; wine and pizza; movies and hamburgers will win your Monkey's heart.

THE LOWE DOWN

Go for it and don't be surprised if you end up getting the big 'M' word!

Verdict: DATE, LOVE, MARRY

Snake and Rooster

Whoop, whoop – this will really work. You have so much in common in every area of your life – work and home. You both get up reasonably early, work hard during the day and need your sleep.

You're both seriously driven at work and love to have a laugh together. You have different strengths which complement each other so well. In fact, together you and your Rooster will be a force to be reckoned with.

I recommend a curry with a few beers; cocktails and sushi; or the movies and a hamburger – any of those will work for you both.

THE LOWE DOWN

Going to the chapel, and you're going to get married! Just saying!

Verdict: DATE, LOVE, MARRY

Snake and Dog

You and your Dog date will love to flirt outrageously with each other but neither of you will try too hard to take this any further.

Your Dog's thinking process is going to be too slow for your liking. You are both planners, but Dog's will take so long to arrive at the same place that you will get bored.

I can only suggest a very short date so perhaps an ice cream, then wave goodbye.

THE LOWE DOWN

Don't agree to any more than one date... trust me nothing will change.

Verdict: DATE – ONCE ONLY

Snake and Pig

This is not going to work. Not now, not ever! Remember the fire and water thing. You will clash badly, and any of your fiery spark will be completely put out by your Pig's water element.

Your Pig will share your love of order but will do things completely differently to you.

No date. Don't go there. This can only go very, very badly.

THE LOWE DOWN

No, no and no.

Verdict: AVOID

THE LOWE DOWN

DATE:

LOVE:

MARRY:

AVOID:

SPECIAL MENTIONS:

Friendzone

Did you know...?

There have been some serious heavy hitters born Snakes including JFK, Indira Gandhi, Benazir Bhutto, Emmanuel Macron and Stephen Hawking.

Some Snakes have really made their mark on the world like Anne Frank, Stephen Hawking, Buzz Aldrin and Roger Bannister.

Imelda Marcos was an example of the self-indulgence of a Snake. She reportedly had 1220 pairs of shoes.

Snakes who know how to dress up when the occasion requires are Zsa Zsa Gabor, Greta Garbo, Brooke Shields, Sarah Jessica Parker and Grace Kelly.

Snakes are never going to stay in mundane, monotonous, or routine jobs.

Snakes must not date other Snakes, or they will face an evening of trying to score points off each other.

Horse

The seventh Chinese sign is Horse.

At first sight:

Horse years	You were born after the Chinese New Year in: 1906, 1918, 1930, 1942, 1954, 1966, 1978, 1990, 2002 or, if you are very young, 2014.
Horse months	Your love mojo is going to be highest in February, June, July and October. From 6th December and 5th January, you are in your clash month!
Horse days	Dust off your best dating gear on Fridays.
Horse hours	Hours to use 11.00-15.00 & 19.00-21.00.
Element	Fire
Top traits	You are one of the four signs that is super lucky in love. If that wasn't enough, you're blessed with great looks. You're a super sociable soul with charisma in spades. And it's not just all of the extrovert stuff you've got going for you – you can be one of the more passionate lovers amongst the Chinese animal signs.

How you're likely to appear on your first date	Powerful dresser with bright colours.
Best colours	Green, Brown and Red, avoid Blue.
Lucky number	Your best numbers are 4 and 9 but 1 just isn't going to work for you.
Lucky direction	Happy days – your best directions are South, Northeast, Southeast & Northwest. Avoid North.

About you...

Horses are articulate and great conversationalists; nothing makes you happier than to know you are the centre of attention. You can often be seen holding court when discussing topics that interest you.

Nothing fazes Horses especially as you're super determined when you have that bit between your teeth. Getting your own way is no problem using your powers of persuasion.

You may be stubborn and don't always take others' advice. That can mean you take actions to your detriment and that you'll regret.

Horses are independent and love freedom, but when you meet your partner in life you will stand by them. Better still you have a way of meeting the right people. As one of the four peach blossom signs you are lucky in love because people can't help falling in love with you.

Horses are very competitive and are often winners in their chosen field.

You are naturally extroverted, and when asked for your opinion you do not hold back with your ideas. Just remember that this can sometimes be overwhelming for the listener.

You educate yourself through travel, which you love. Just getting in a car or a plane on the way to a new destination ignites your passion.

You always have a clear goal in mind and keep that constantly in sight. Your superpower is organisation. However, it's great to remember that you are on fire and not everyone can keep up with your speed.

You're passionate and caring towards your friends and family. You're sensitive and your unselfish ways mean that sometimes you can be taken for granted a little, but you're okay with that. You love unconditionally – until someone crosses your boundaries.

You're intuitive and love to surround yourself with intuitive people who get you.

Horses love being around people, but that doesn't mean you don't enjoy me-time. You love to lose yourself in a book or a documentary. You're a bit of a soft touch when it comes to movies and the odd romcom.

At school you are studious but once you leave school then you are a rule-breaking, party animal. As you get older, you'll love your home and have people over for dinner and parties regularly. You love good food, wine and socialising. In fact, you can be guilty of all of the vices if you're not tamed early.

You are made for sales, accountancy, entertaining and writing. You'd be an excellent barrister as well. You'll hate monotonous jobs where you have to do the same thing every day, or don't have the chance to use your skills and abilities. Any job where you get to make presentations is great for Horses.

Your superpowers in work and business are your charm, common sense, strategic ideas, and the ability to complete everything you start. Your weaknesses are that you are very opinionated and outspoken with your ideas, and you don't listen to others enough.

Career will have your focus more than your home. You will struggle being at home all of the time, because it will feel boring. That said, your home will feel like a home. Your home will be somewhere that when you walk in you feel instantly relaxed. You may have ancestral or antique pieces that have been handed down to you. Horses love paintings and cushions, with loads of family pictures on the walls.

Happily, Horses love exercise. Some of you will choose to run daily or hit the gym. When you get started on that run or arrive at the gym you will get your head down and get it done, but your efforts can come in fits and starts. You are into fitness and with a medium build your weight can yo-yo and your appearance is important to you. When you feel like you're putting on weight you will focus hard on losing it and can be quite controlled.

In terms of whether you like being at home or outside, you are pretty balanced on this point. You like both. Being outside in a pretty garden will make you happy, but when it gets cold, you'll want to be curled up in front of an open fire. You have no trouble getting up in the morning and getting on with your day, even if you've partied well into the night.

Horses love money and know how to spend it, but it's unlikely to be on cars. Even if you fancy a flash car you won't be able to fit your friends or you're shopping in it so it won't work. You're really a simple soul but you know what clothes suit you and when you need to up the ante in the dressing stakes.

It's time to talk about love...

Horses prefer to be in relationships and are not afraid of PDAs and cuddles with the right person. They want to be married for life, but if they're with the wrong person they will end the relationship and set off to find their soulmate.

You want someone who is passionate, loves family, wants to hit the town, and have a good time. Horses want a lover who will spoil them and loves travelling. You need a strong-minded soul who knows where they are going in life. Your partner is going to need to have their own career or there is a serious risk that you'll get bored. My best bet is that not only will you want kids, but you'll have two or three.

Your ideal dates are going to be at a theatre, fine restaurants and long walks along the beach. But you're also up for cooking courses and action days.

The lucky person dating you can expect that you'll be on time, appropriately dressed for whatever type of date you've opted for. You'll be attentive, flirty, funny, and easily keep their interest. For your part you will need some excitement and for them to keep your interest.

Horses are super-organised with their dating. Beware though that you can be a bit pushy booking dates ahead, even as far as months beforehand. You don't want to chase your perfect partner away.

You don't mind one-night stands. Horses love sex and being sexy. But once you are in the right relationship, you will remain loyal.

So, let's get down to business and tell you which signs in the Chinese Horoscopes you should date, love, marry or avoid.

Let's talk about love...

Horse and Rat

If you like a fiery relationship, then this is the one. You will debate everything and anything. You will clash. Your element is Fire and your Rat's element is Water. You always want to be the centre of attention and your Rat will want to take the floor in certain circumstances and you won't like that.

You will always want to control your Rat, and less than surprisingly they won't like that much.

A bar with karaoke will work for both of you – you can both be the centre of attention.

THE LOWE DOWN

The only way this can work as a relationship is if you are okay with constant clashes and giving up centre stage every now and then. Nope – I didn't think so.

Verdict: AVOID

Horse and Ox

This is not a match made in heaven. You're way too strong for the gentle Ox. You'll completely dominate them which won't work for either of you.

You live your life at different speeds. You are on fast forward whereas your Ox will much prefer to plod along and take time to notice the scenery.

I recommend not going on a date, but if you want to give it a try then perhaps watch the film about the Tortoise and the Hare.

THE LOWE DOWN

This will not be a fun date or a healthy, balanced relationship.

Verdict: AVOID

Horse and Tiger

Yes, yes, and yes! You have found your soulmate in your Tiger. You are both strong characters and will bounce off each other. Your Tiger will be the support crew and you will happily drag your Tiger behind you as you go off on your many adventures. Your Tiger will definitely not complain.

Your romance will be a whirlwind. I suggest you take them to a rock concert. You'll both love that! An Escape Room would also get both of your pulses racing.

THE LOWE DOWN

There is a strong possibility for marriage.

Verdict: DATE, LOVE, MARRY

Horse and Rabbit

There is no potential for a love match here. You want the spotlight, and your Rabbit will be left in the shadows. You won't stop for breath to give them time to enjoy the journey.

If you still want to go on a date then take them on a dog walk in the country, with a picnic and a nice bottle of vino. You might be bored but your Rabbit will enjoy themselves.

THE LOWE DOWN

This match won't take off.

Verdict: FRIENDZONE

Horse and Dragon

You'll make the decisions in this match. You have magical powers over your Dragon. They won't be happy about it because, as we all know, Dragons are magical.

Choose somewhere crazy and quirky to take your Dragon. Something like banger racing where you race in beat-up old cars would work or maybe an early afternoon hot air balloon ride.

THE LOWE DOWN

Nope this is not for you.

Verdict: DATE, FRIENDZONE

Horse and Snake

You both love a spreadsheet. That could sound unkind, but it won't to you two. You could talk figures every day. You'll both grab the bill at the end of a dinner date hoping to find a mistake.

Just a word of warning on this match. You are both fire signs, so avoid subjects you might argue about!

This is going to friendzone itself but if you decide to try out a date before that I suggest you pick some sort of challenge. A murder mystery or a pub quiz would leave both of you feeling smug about winning.

THE LOWE DOWN

This will stay squarely in the friendzone and you'll both be happy with that.

Verdict: FRIENDZONE

Horse and Horse

You are a passionate mix, and you will end up in bed whatever you do. You are on fire in that area but that is literally the only thing you won't be competitive about.

You both want to be winners in whatever you do, and you have very strong views which could be the undoing of you both.

I don't recommend that you take your Horse on a date. If you do, then just get a room and sow your wild oats. You will both love that.

THE LOWE DOWN

Once you get out of bed and have to speak to each other those other types of sparks will fly. It will be constant and exhausting.

Verdict: AVOID

Horse and Goat

Love, love, love – you are an amazing team! You and your Goat will complement each other in so many ways.

You bring the passion, and your Goat will bring the contentment. You bring out the best in each other so I would say this is a match made in heaven.

As you are an awesome team and both like to win, I suggest a date where there is some sort of competition you can take part in together and win, win, win!

THE LOWE DOWN

You really would make a great team in marriage.

Verdict: DATE, LOVE, MARRY, MARRY, MARRY

Horse and Monkey

Whoop! The adrenaline will be flying with this match. You both crave excitement and adventure and anything that fuels that will work for you.

Just a tiny caution here – you are going to egg each other on big time so be sure that whatever you do has a safety net. You'll be queuing for the scary rides at a fun fair or bungee jumping, and both will work.

THE LOWE DOWN

Fun and memorable, but nothing here to form a solid relationship.

Verdict: DATE, FRIENDZONE

Horse and Rooster

You will control your Rooster. This will come as a surprise because Roosters well and truly know their own minds.

You love order and so do Roosters, but as soon as your Rooster sees something with more shine, they will disappear.

This is not a match on any level, but if you insist on trying a date consider an outside BBQ where you can look like you're together but keep a safe distance.

Give it a miss!

THE LOWE DOWN

This is not going to work on any level.

Verdict: AVOID

Horse and Dog

You two are mates for life. You have so much in common. You both love travelling and day trips to check out new places.

There is just no passion between you and so it's not worth pursuing this relationship unless of course you just want a friendship.

For a date perhaps zip down to the coast for fish and chips on the beach.

THE LOWE DOWN

It will be fun but it won't come to anything.

Verdict: FRIENDZONE

Horse and Pig

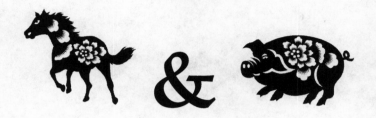

Wow, this mix could really work. Your brains are a great match, and you are both excellent businesspeople. You will bond over excellent PowerPoint presentations.

Marriage would also mean though that you both need your own space… but you would both be fine with that.

You could find yourself heading to the same training course or a workshop on NLP. You both love that stuff. Follow it up with excellent wine in a fancy wine bar and you will impress your Pig.

THE LOWE DOWN

Yep, this is going to be a fantastic match.

Verdict: DATE, LOVE, MARRY

THE LOWE DOWN

DATE:

LOVE:

MARRY:

AVOID:

SPECIAL MENTIONS:

Friendzone

Heavenly match

Did you know...?

Perhaps one of the world's greatest ever leaders, Nelson Mandela, was a Goat. Other Horse politicians include Joe Biden, Angela Merkel, Anwar Sadat and Condoleezza Rice.

Some mighty Horse women who are influencing the world are Greta Thunberg and Emma Watson.

More controversial Horse politicians have included Kim Jong-Il and Muammar Gaddafi.

Amongst famous Horses are some serious heavy hitters in the music industry like Aretha Franklin, Ray Charles, Tammy Wynette, Brian Wilson, Usher, Sinéad O'Connor and Barbra Streisand.

Horses are not underrepresented in acting either. Just a few of them are John Travolta, Sean Connery, Margot Robbie, Katie Holmes, Salma Hayek, Halle Berry, Luke Perry, Denzel Washington and Gene Hackman.

Horses love change and action, so they are way too much for placid, kind-hearted Oxen.

Goat

The eighth Chinese Horoscope sign is Goat.

At first sight:

Goat years	You were born after the Chinese New Year in: 1919, 1931, 1943, 1955, 1967, 1979, 1991, 2003, 2015.
Goat months	Your love mojo is going to be highest in February, June, July and November. Avoid travelling 4th January to 3rd February.
Goat days	Dust off your best dating gear on Sunday.
Goat hours	Goat's best hours 11.00-15.00; they can come alive 21.00-23.00.
Element	Earth
Top traits	Goats are negotiators, they have endless patience, they are kind and trustworthy. They are no fools so don't take them for one.

How you're likely to appear on your first date	Have their own styles, they may not have changed it since they were teenagers.
Best colours	You'll rock Red, Pink and earthy colours but ditch the grey, it makes you feel gloomy.
Lucky number	Your best number is 9 but 7 just isn't going to work for you.
Lucky direction	Happy days, your best directions are South, Northwest & Southwest. Northeast isn't the direction you want to be heading.

First let's talk about you...

Goats make great companions in life. Your superpower is that you know how to negotiate. You will always make sure your opinion is heard before any partnership decisions are made.

You give great advice, but people will have to ask you for it. Your gentle nature doesn't allow you to push yourself forward unless you see bullying. Bullying is one of your pet hates.

You prefer to go with the flow, you're not a lover of structure, and timekeeping definitely isn't one of your strengths.

You're super sensitive, and you can get depressed if you're criticised, which can make you more introverted. This is part of your make-up. You're happier in a library or somewhere quiet where you can write poetry and ponder the world without being affected by the negative news that is all around us.

You do have opinions and you find a way to communicate them without causing offence or arguments. Literally one of your other superpowers is that you're a peacemaker. You can be intuitive and have learned to listen to your inner voice and use it wisely.

While growing up and at school you were studious with beautiful writing. Your books and files would all have been neat, tidy and completely in order. If you had prefects at your school, you would've been asked to be one. You might have knocked the offer back though, because you don't like the limelight.

You need to be around people. You don't mind short periods of time by yourself, but you'd have to know that you had plans to see people later in the day. You're not really a party animal though. You prefer small groups of people, ideally no more than six at a time.

You may love a glass of wine and a bit of music while you're chatting with people, but you're not really inclined to overdo it. You like eating healthy food but you can be enticed to overindulge. Well obviously, there are exceptions!

Goats love a holiday in the sun where you can relax and enjoy the sun on your bones while reading a romantic novel or alternatively a best-seller. You don't want to miss out on anything.

Goats are not great at getting up in the morning. You're slow starting so best not to put anything in your diary before 10 o'clock or chances are you'll be completely disorganised and have last night's make-up still on.

Goats do not love exercise. You will start exercising in a gym, but you won't keep it up because it just doesn't interest you. Fitness and being in shape don't really matter to you once you've met your partner for life.

You make great librarians, poets, writers, and police negotiators. You'd also be great at human resources. You want to save the world so anything that involves creativity, interaction with people or is humanitarian is a great option for you. Don't apply for a job in sales, it's just not your bag.

Your superpowers at work or in business are the ability to listen to others and to support them in their endeavours. You have the capacity to see all points of view in a discussion. Your weakness is that you don't like structure or routine.

You are a career and a home type. You value both and balance them well. Your home will be homely, and it is your happy place. Your kitchen is probably a bit untidy with some unwashed dishes in the sink, but the upside is that there will always be lovely aromas coming from that same kitchen. Your bedroom is very likely to be messy but lived in.

You will make an excellent parent. Literally as soon as you can in your relationship, you'll want kids and be very involved in their lives from when they're babies, until they are old. You'll be inclined to take on your children's woes, physically and mentally, and their joyful and happy times.

Cars are not important to you. If you do decide on a well-known brand, it's more likely to be an older version. That doesn't mean that you don't appreciate a nice-looking sports car, just that you don't have to own it.

Fashion isn't really something important to you. You tend to stick to the fashions you're familiar with. What you wear might be what you grew up in or influenced by what your parents wear. You're not a fussy dresser but you know how to match colours together.

It's time to talk about love…

Your perfect dates are likely to be music festivals, country walks, movies, binge-watching Netflix at home on the sofa or dance classes with friends. You prefer places you can talk and hear each other. Romantic dinners are great as well. Chances are you'll choose a coffee catch-up to make sure that they are the right person.

Your date can expect you to be late for everything. You are completely disorganised, but your perfect date will forgive you. It's best if they give you a 30-minute warning. You will be chatty and the people you're with will be very interested in anything you have to say. You prefer chilled-out dates. You will not be up for parachute jumping.

It's hard to imagine how persuasive someone would have to be to convince you into a one-night stand. You're a faithful type so it won't sit completely comfortably.

Goats are lucky in love, and you won't commit until you're sure. When you find your soulmate, you will marry for life and love being part of a family. Goats prefer to be in relationships, rather than single. Oddly, Goats can look for someone who has been married before as a potential love partner and you'll prefer someone who can balance career with home life.

To be your perfect love partner your date is going to need to be kind, adaptable, family-oriented, and laid-back. An all-round good egg will be your type. They'll have to like cuddles as well because you are touchy-feely and will return the favour.

So, let's get down to business and tell you which signs in the Chinese Horoscopes you should date, love, marry or avoid.

Let's talk about love...
Goat and Rat

This is an interesting mix. You have a lot in common but there's also a lot that could irritate you about each other. You're a quiet, peaceful animal whereas your Rat will never stop talking.

The glue that will keep you together is your love of family and you'll both make extremely good parents. At home your Rat will tend to be quieter and relaxed, so harmony will abound.

Your Rat will love a date somewhere sociable, with others around. A friend's party or a group outing to a local pizzeria would really work.

THE LOWE DOWN

Marriage is on the cards for these two with love and happiness in the mix.

Verdict: DATE, LOVE, MARRY

Goat and Ox

To be honest this is not a great match. You both have a wee stubborn streak, which could end up in fiery arguments. Usually, you get along with the other Chinese zodiac animals but not so much with each other.

Perhaps a quick cup of tea – on second thoughts perhaps make it a takeout tea, so you can both go your own ways quickly.

THE LOWE DOWN

Don't even go there for a date. This match won't work.

Verdict: AVOID

Goat and Tiger

You're a gentle soul and like a quieter, more carefree life. Your Tiger, however, is playful and doesn't know how to sit still for long. They need to be busy all of the time.

This isn't a perfect match, but you will learn a lot from each other.

Your first date could be taking your Tiger for a walk around a garden centre. You can take time to check out the plants and flowers and your Tiger can entertain themselves pushing all of the buttons on the garden gadgets and water features.

THE LOWE DOWN

This isn't going to go anywhere but you'll enjoy your date.

Verdict: DATE

Goat and Rabbit

From the minute you meet you will hit it off with your Rabbit. It will feel as though you've known each other forever. You have so much in common it will feel like serendipity. You might even find that you've been in the same places at the same time throughout your lives.

Will this match work? Hell yes! It's straight down the wedding aisle for you two.

You won't need my help to find dates to charm your Rabbit because whatever you choose, your Rabbit will be excited about it. My suggestion is to make it somewhere quiet enough to hear each other talk.

THE LOWE DOWN

Oh yes, you can definitely put a ring on your Rabbit's finger.

Verdict: DATE, LOVE, MARRY

Goat and Dragon

This match is a non-starter. There's no spark, no passion and even less hope for a future together.

You are both very kind and gentle so I can see you both agreeing to a date just to avoid letting the other down.

My recommendation is not to bother dating. You will be bored, and you'll have to find an excuse to leave without offending your Dragon.

THE LOWE DOWN

Boredom isn't the basis for a date, let alone a relationship.

Verdict: AVOID

Goat and Snake

You are a team player and Snakes are not! They can be secretive, and frankly they'll be too controlling for your gentle Goat nature.

You probably know this and so will your Snake because you're both so intuitive. And as a result of that intuition, you'll probably both also know that this relationship is a non-starter.

A date using your crystal ball to see into the future if your intuition lets you down. Oh, you don't have one. Sorry, but you'll work it out sooner rather than later.

THE LOWE DOWN

Give it a miss!

Verdict: AVOID

Goat and Horse

I can hear the music playing for your wedding as I write this. You two complement each other on so many levels. You're both team players and with your Horse you have found the perfect partner to win at life.

You bring gentleness and compassion, and your Horse brings the passion and energy – what a great mix!

A fantastic date option would be something like a bowling alley where you can chatter to your hearts' content. By the way – the chances are you will have the same scores at the end of your date.

THE LOWE DOWN

You two can make a great love team.

Verdict: DATE, LOVE, MARRY

Goat and Goat

Wow, you two really are a match made in heaven. You two are so incredibly compatible. It's literally boring to watch you together, you are so blissfully happy. You're both blessed with negotiating skills and will each want to please the other.

Take your Goat anywhere that you will enjoy, and they will love it too. Country walks, romantic dinners, anything really. It will work.

THE LOWE DOWN

You can start planning your wedding day.

Verdict: DATE, LOVE, MARRY

Goat and Monkey

You bring stability and certainty to your Monkey. They, in turn, will bring out your fun, playful side. In short, they will bring joy into your life.

You can treat your Monkey to somewhere fancy or let them take you on an adventure for some adrenaline pumping experience, like paragliding.

THE LOWE DOWN

This is a really good balance. You two can definitely form a lifetime partnership.

Verdict: DATE, LOVE, MARRY

Goat and Rooster

You will talk, talk, and talk some more with your Rooster. You have loads in common. Your Rooster will share your passion for life and you're both kind and caring.

Sadly, there will be no passion for each other, but that's okay because you have found a friend for life.

I suggest hitting a bar or a gin, whiskey or vodka tasting event. After that your Rooster will love an Italian meal.

THE LOWE DOWN

It's not going to become a relationship, but you'll enjoy shooting the breeze with your Rooster.

Verdict: DATE, FRIENDZONE

Goat and Dog

No, no and no! I can't stress enough that this will not work. You are both far too stubborn and if you don't get your own way, you'll both sulk.

The Dog is not the best communicator, and the Goat loves to talk.

No point taking about a potential date here, it will be a disaster.

THE LOWE DOWN

You get the picture: unless your idea of fun is sulking your way through a date, give it a miss.

Verdict: AVOID

Goat and Pig

This could really work. You develop a friendship quickly and this is one of those that really could turn into love and marriage.

You'd have to be happy with your Pig being the boss. They're going to be making the decisions and you'll go along with it because you love them.

Sushi followed by an art gallery, an exhibition or a museum would work for both of you.

THE LOWE DOWN

If you don't mind your Pig making the decisions, then get those wedding invites out there.

Verdict: DATE, LOVE, MARRY

THE LOWE DOWN

DATE:

LOVE:

MARRY:

AVOID:

SPECIAL MENTIONS:

Friendzone

Did you know...?

There are a lot of Goats in politics around the world including John Major, John Kerry, Mikhail Gorbachev, Nicolas Sarkozy, Pervez Musharraf, Newt Gingrich, Raul Castro, Christine Lagarde and Paul Keating.

Some Goats have changed the world like Tim Berners-Lee.

More than a few Goats have reached dizzying heights in business like Steve Jobs and Bill Gates.

Goats are a good-looking lot such as Nicole Kidman and her amour Keith Urban, Jason Momoa and Julia Roberts.

Superstar Goats include Whoopi Goldberg, Heath Ledger, Leonard Nimoy, Mick Jagger, Toni Morrison, John Wayne, Nat King Cole, Robert De Niro, Laurence Olivier, Keith Richards and Katharine Hepburn.

It's easy to see that Goats like Kurt Cobain and Noel Gallagher would not be fans of structure and routine.

Monkey

The ninth Chinese animal sign is Monkey.

At first sight:

Monkey years	You were born after the Chinese New Year in: 1910, 1920, 1932, 1944, 1956, 1968, 1980, 1992, 2004 or, if you are very young, 2016.
Monkey months	Your love mojo is going to be highest in April, May, August and December. From 6th December to 5th January, you are going to be on fire!
Monkey days	Dust off your best dating gear on Saturdays.
Monkey hours	Monkeys are hottest between 9-11am, 3-5pm and 11pm-1am.
Element	Metal
Top traits	Have a multitude of talents. They are creative and inventive, quick-witted, and a little devious.

How you're likely to appear on your first date	Smart but casual. Of course, it depends on the type of date as Monkeys can adapt easily.
Best colours	You'll rock white, grey, blue and black with a bit of pink or red but ditch the green it will kill the mood.
Lucky number	Your best numbers are 8 and 6, but 1 just isn't going to work for you.
Lucky direction	Happy days your best directions are Southeast, North & West. Northeast isn't the direction you want to be heading.

Let's talk about you...

You cheeky Monkeys are the top Chinese animals to have fun with, so people will always be giving you a call to book time out to catch up with you. If they're feeling blue then you will support them, give them great advice, and always have their backs. You're a good friend to have.

As a Monkey you're quick-witted and love to share your sense of humour even it does include a swear word or three. You are so sharp-witted it's hard to catch up when you make one joke after another.

You're resourceful and you always know someone to call in a crisis. If your best friend needs a plumber, electrician or accountant your phone will be full of amazing people to help your friends out.

Your imagination makes you a great storyteller, and people love to hear about your adventures from childhood to adult life. Do you exaggerate in your storytelling, probably a little, but that's okay.

You can be a little cunning and devious, but hey, no one is perfect.

Super creative and often attracted to art, you have an eye for colour so make fantastic interior designers and painters. You can tell a Monkey a secret but beware that you might find a remarkably similar story in one of their novels. You draw a lot of inspiration from being around people and people want to spend time with you. You are super curious and have a thirst for adventure.

Fairness and justice are critically important to Monkeys, so you'll likely be attracted to a career as a solicitor or barrister, fighting for the underdog every time. These jobs will work well for your sensitive Monkey soul.

You're great with figures but have the capacity to spend everything you have on yourself, family and friends. You are so generous that sometimes you turn your pockets out and moths fly out.

You can be a little pushy, opinionated sometimes, especially when life is treating you and the ones you love unfairly.

With anyone who has clown tendencies... oh didn't I say before that you were probably the classroom clown – you can suffer from depression, and you need to learn to share those dark moments with your family and friends. They can then happily repay you for all of the times you have been there for them.

At school, you're usually studious but are very likely to get told off for talking too much. If your BFF leads you into rule breaking, you will willingly follow. So, chances are that you spent some time in detention.

You are very sensitive, with a huge heart and you will empathise with others. Monkeys have the capacity to be intuitive, but you will need to work on it. Funnily enough Monkeys come across as extroverts, but there is a very definite introvert inside trying to get out. You love to be around people but your own time to think is essential.

You love food, wine and music. In your younger years your curiosity might lead you to experiment with drugs and alcohol, but as you get older, you'll be just as happy with a cup of tea and a chinwag. You're well up for a party but you'd be just as happy to be a homebody.

You might want to sit on a beach but you're unlikely to be up for climbing Mount Everest. Now, I'm not saying you're lazy... but what is a gym? Swimming, yes, you're familiar with that word and you will indulge in a pool from time to time.

As I said earlier Monkeys are not gym bunnies. If you need to lose weight limiting your food will be preferable to having to exercise for fitness. You won't be into meditation because you're not allowed to chat.

You are a bit yin/yang on the career or home preference. You're equally happy with both. Monkeys work well in creative jobs. Interior designers, decorators and writers are great choices. You could equally find your place as a travel consultant, solicitor, or engineer. You will hate mundane jobs.

Your superpowers at work are your creativity and empathy for others. But you can be too spontaneous and need to do some long-term planning.

A Monkey's home is going to be stylish and fairly tidy. That's not to say that there isn't clutter in some areas, like the kitchen. There will always be a drawer that needs clearing out. You're also stylish and fashionable in what you choose to wear.

You do love to dress to impress, and you're not frightened of bringing colour into your wardrobe. If you're with a partner, you will synchronise your dress unintentionally. When you choose your partner, it can be as if you become one intuitively.

You're perfectly happy with practical cars but that doesn't mean you wouldn't love a fancy car like a Range Rover Evoque.

It's time to talk about love...

Monkeys prefer to be in relationships and when they get married it's for life. You are happy with or without children if you are in the right relationship. Roosters can be similar; they can take or leave having children. You're not really one for one-night stands unless you've imbibed too much alcohol.

Monkeys need someone with intelligence, someone that is loyal, trustworthy and that you can have fun with. You're not going to put up with stupid people who open their mouths and look like idiots. Shared values in life are critical and communication is really important to you, it must be two-way. You're a curious person so you need your partner to be up for experiencing new things and to be great travel companions. In turn, you are fiercely loyal and will stick with your love through thick and thin, and your love will get someone generous with cuddles. You are very organised when it comes to your love life. You'll always remember your anniversary and your love's birthday.

Your best date options are going to depend on your mood. You love food and wine so a lovely meal in a restaurant is a great option. You like shopping, parties, going to the theatre or a recital, the movies or even a concert. Once you get to know someone better a cosy night in with a good bottle of wine and Netflix will also suit you well.

Your date can expect someone who is stylish and dresses well for whatever date you're going on. You'll be super chatty and flirty. Your chat will be intelligent though, because you're across the latest news and you're not short on opinions. You're usually on time and don't really appreciate people who are late to a party.

So, let's get down to business and tell you which signs in the Chinese Horoscopes you should date, love, marry or avoid.

Let's talk about love...

Monkey and Rat

The upside to this match is that you and your Rat complement each other. You wake up at the same time, you enjoy your afternoons together and you both know how to paint the town red at night. Together you are a sexy couple. You're going to have trouble keeping your hands off each other, even in public.

There is going to be a lot of 'dessert' happening in this relationship, so save time and get a room.

THE LOWE DOWN

The problem is that Rats like to talk and talk and talk, and you may find that really draining. Still if your Rat learns when to shut up this could turn into marriage.

Verdict: DATE, LOVE, MARRY

Monkey and Ox

This is a great match. You are the cheeky and adventurous type, and you will bring the fun side out in your Ox. You'll even manage to stop them working all the time. Your Ox will create a loving home for you to come back to and you will love that.

You two love doing stuff together so why don't you take your Ox to a pizza or sushi making class, and after you've eaten your creations, whisk them off for a few drinks.

THE LOWE DOWN

Marriage is a definite possibility for you two. You bring out the best in each other.

Verdict: DATE, LOVE, MARRY

Monkey and Tiger

Wow, all I can say is avoid, avoid, avoid! You two will clash big time. Your element is metal, and your Tiger's is wood. You're both very strong characters, and while you both enjoy having fun, this is not a win-win situation and neither of you like to lose.

You could take your Tiger clay pigeon shooting but beware of being tempted to turn the guns on each other.

THE LOWE DOWN

Don't go there. Trust me!

Verdict: AVOID

Monkey and Rabbit

You and your Rabbit share a fantastic sense of humour. You'll have so much fun with your Rabbit and there will be so much fun and laughter, always.

Although fun is at the top of your list you also share values. You both put family first and remember that not all family is blood related. When you marry your friends will always be popping round to see you both and you'll be okay with that.

I suggest taking your Rabbit to a comedy show so you can laugh together all night.

THE LOWE DOWN

This one can end up in marriage and will be a laugh a minute.

Verdict: DATE, LOVE, MARRY

Monkey and Dragon

This match is an interesting one. Date, Love, Marry or Friendzone! You will spend so much time chatting that you might forget to move from the Friendzone to the next step.

You and your Dragon bring out the kid in each other, so a date at a fun fair or carnival where you can eat candy floss and ice cream and be silly will work for both of you.

THE LOWE DOWN

OR

You could end up going to the chapel and getting married, or just great friends. Either way your date will be fun.

Verdict: DATE, LOVE, MARRY OR FRIENDZONE

Monkey and Snake

This is also an odd and slightly unpredictable match. You will be BFFs with your Snake and get along on most things, except politics. Really, do NOT discuss politics!

This relationship could turn into marriage; you'll both have different roles to play but you complement each other in so many ways. You'll know within the first few minutes whether you're going to be BFFs or get married. You both have intuition so use it!

Some great date choices that will work for your Snake are coffee and cake, wine and pizza, burgers and movies or a Netflix binge. All of these are a great plan.

THE LOWE DOWN

Okay so you could end up marrying your Snake BFF or it could just be a few dates.

OR

Verdict: DATE, LOVE, MARRY OR FRIENDZONE

Monkey and Horse

You two will have fun together, especially if you do something adventurous. I can see you both auditioning for the *Fast & Furious* movies. But this date is as far as this match will go. There's no scope for a relationship here.

If auditions for Hollywood blockbusters aren't an option, any date that gets the adrenaline pumping will work for both of you.

Think lessons to fly helicopters, the most heart-pumping rides at a local theme park or parasailing. You will both love any of these options.

THE LOWE DOWN

You'll remember your date forever, but you'll end up friend-zoning your Horse.

Verdict: DATE, FRIENDZONE

Monkey and Goat

Yep, this is a win-win relationship. It will probably end in marriage, but it might be a long courtship. You'll be up for getting a ring on it quickly, but your Goat will take their time because they want everything to be perfect.

You are great for your Goat. You'll bring out their fun side in spades and you will love the stability they bring to your life.

I recommend going out for a meal. Try ordering each other's meals – that will make both of you laugh.

THE LOWE DOWN

This is a well-balanced match and could go the whole way.

Verdict: DATE, LOVE, MARRY

Monkey and Monkey

Oh wow, this is going to get messy! Two fun, cheeky Monkeys together.

What you will get up to together is unmentionable; luckily you can both keep secrets.

How about making a video as you go around a zoo? Don't forget to take selfies with the monkeys though! Then off to a burger joint to top it all off. You'll have so much fun.

THE LOWE DOWN

You will have the best date together, but you're too similar. You might stretch to another date but it's not going to work long-term.

Verdict: DATE

Monkey and Rooster

You two are great pals. You just can't stop talking. It doesn't really matter where you go, you'll just keep talking.

You are both great in business and while you are together you will come up with some wacky ideas on how to make money.

Hit the pubs or a café (preferably with wine and cheese) for your date. Make sure it's somewhere you can chat and hear each other though.

THE LOWE DOWN

You will enjoy each other's company so much that you'll stay great friends.

Verdict: FRIENDZONE

Monkey and Dog

Your Dog enjoys the finer things in life, and you are well up for that. You know how to show your Dog a great time and you will.

A fancy place like The Ivy or The Ritz for a posh afternoon tea. Anywhere you can dress up in your fancy gear will work too.

THE LOWE DOWN

This could go the distance.

Verdict: DATE, LOVE, MARRY

Monkey and Pig

You two will grate on each other badly. You just won't be able to see each other's good points. You are at opposite ends on some things. Your Pig will see you as 'all over the place' and you will consider them positively OCD.

Don't bother going on a date – it won't work.

THE LOWE DOWN

This isn't even going to get off the ground.

Verdict: AVOID

THE LOWE DOWN

DATE:

LOVE:

Monkey

MARRY:

AVOID:

SPECIAL MENTIONS:

Friendzone

Did you know...?

There are some very mighty Monkey women and just a few are Jacinda Ardern, Diana Ross, Martina Navratilova, Elizabeth Taylor, Bette Davis and Kylie Minogue.

Music legend Bob Marley was a Monkey.

It's easier to name the actors who aren't Monkeys but here are a few who are – Hugh Jackman, Tom Hanks, Jennifer Aniston, Daniel Craig, Michael Douglas, Lucy Lawless, Tom Selleck, Kim Cattrall, Elijah Wood and Owen Wilson.

Musicians abound in the Monkey world – Cardi B, Zayn Malik, Christina Aguilera, Joe Cocker, Demi Lovato, Dave Grohl and Jessica Simpson.

Sport is another area where Monkeys excel including Venus Williams, Bjorn Borg and Michael Schumacher.

Monkeys can be sociable, but Rats can drain them easily with too much chat.

Rooster

The tenth Chinese animal sign is Rooster.

At first sight:

Rooster years	You were born after the Chinese New Year in: 1921, 1933, 1945, 1957, 1969, 1981, 1993, 2005 or, if you are very young, 2017.
Rooster months	Your love mojo is going to be highest in April, May and September. From 5th January, you are going to be on fire!
Rooster days	Dust off your best dating gear on Fridays.
Rooster hours	You are an early bird and your favourite times of the day 07.00-11.00 and then come alive at 17.00-19.00.
Element	Metal
Top traits	Trustworthy, Honourable, Flamboyant, Hardworking, Stylish, and they are one of the four Peach Blossoms so you can't help falling in love with them.

How you're likely to appear on your first date	Confident, outgoing manner, stylish and they love to socialise.
Best colours	You'll rock blue, black, and pink, but ditch the green it will kill the mood.
Lucky number	Your best numbers are 6 & 8, but 2 just isn't going to work for you.
Lucky direction	Happy days, your best directions are Northeast & Southeast. East isn't the direction you want to be heading.

About you...

Roosters are reliable. They are the person to go to if someone needs something. They are also very trustworthy if you have a secret. They'll keep your secret even if they're tortured, so your confidences are safe with them.

You are super hardworking and you're great with deadlines because you are conscientious and care about what you do. Roosters start work early just like their namesake. Nothing annoys a Rooster more than people not pulling their weight on a work project or at home. If you are up, then whoever you are dating will need to be up as well.

You are much more suited to working for yourself, but you can be a CEO or hold another high-level position in a company. You are a natural leader socially and professionally. You're methodical, so your finances are always in order. Even if you look messy, you know what you're doing.

You are honourable and generous, often giving both money and time to charities without others knowing.

One of your top skills is finding and taking opportunities to enhance your life and the lives of others around you.

You're an opinionated extrovert and love to be in the middle of a discussion about putting the world to rights. I'm not saying you're an activist and you're going to chain yourself to railings, but if there is a way of keeping the peace and doing what is needed to make the world a better place then you'll put your hand up to be involved.

At school you were a rule breaker and regularly in detention, usually for chatting too much. Chances are you spent most of your time looking out of the window during maths, chemistry and biology but loved English literature and business studies.

In your younger years you are a bit of a party person and a rebel. But as you get older and settle into a relationship, you're likely to be less about alcohol and partying, and more couples orientated. You're a great yin/yang balance in that you like being at home and out in equal measure. So, you're a party animal but you love your time at home as well, and you'll go through times of doing both. You do know how to party, and you shine in social groups.

Fitness isn't high on your agenda, but if you feel unfit then you will look at your diet and take some extra walks. The gym is likely to be a word you really don't like but you love being out in the country and doing activities there.

Roosters are sensitive with others, but you can often forget to look after yourself. You're intuitive in your personal and professional lives but you really need to believe in yourself. Careers that would work for you are anything creative, the law, party planning, property investment, metaphysics, engineering, and professional speaking.

You'd rather start work early and finish early, but you may go back and do some work later. Your professional superpowers are in strategic planning and you're trustworthy. Your weaknesses are that sometimes your decisions get you into trouble, because even though you're a planner you're also a risk taker.

You are inclined to put your career before your home life. You may become a parent, but you'll still continue to be dedicated to your career. You will help your children understand about life from being streetwise to higher education.

When choosing a partner, you're very likely to choose a partner who values their career and family as much as you do.

People are very important to you. As I said before, you do like your downtime, but you will generally have the TV or radio on in the background.

You really appreciate and enjoy good food and wine and fast, fancy cars and labels and brands appeal to you as well. It's all about the style, but you won't buy to impress others, you do it to make yourself happy. You tend to follow fashion and you really know what suits you. You're likely to be a bit sassy in how you dress.

Roosters take pride in their homes and they're generally stylish and minimalistic. Your flair for design can be seen throughout your house in your collection of pictures, mirrors, and clocks. It would be very unusual for you to paint your walls different colours throughout your house because you can be a little OCD when it comes to decorating your home.

Let's talk about love...

Roosters have a passion for love. You're one of the four peach blossoms of the Chinese animals which makes you particularly lucky in love, alongside Rabbits, Rats and Horses.

Roosters can tend to be a bit fickle because you fall in love easily. You may even be engaged a few times before you settle down and get married. As I've said before, you are both Yin and Yang: you're happy in a relationship and being single.

When people are in a relationship with you, they soon learn that cuddles are mainly for behind closed doors. You're not one to be overly affectionate in public. But you will hug friends as a hello.

If you find the right partner, then you can marry for life. That does depend on their capacity to continually show their love.

Roosters need to be appreciated and can be very demanding in a relationship.

So, what are you looking for? Loyalty and trustworthiness are critical. You want someone who enjoys the good things in life. You don't suffer fools so you need someone who can hold a conversation but won't show them up. You will be loyal to your love partner but that doesn't mean that you won't be flirty.

You'll love dates in restaurants, concerts, theatre, exhibitions, and anything that involves dancing. Catching up with friends will also work. Your date can expect you to be on time and dressed just right for wherever you're going. Your date is in for a treat as you can be a bit sexy, flirty and chatty. Your date will need to engage with you for you to enjoy it and they'll need to be organised and punctual or you'll be saying bye-bye to them.

So, let's get down to business and tell you which signs in the Chinese Horoscopes you should date, love, marry or avoid.

Let's talk about love...

Rooster and Rat

This is not a match made in heaven. Roosters are early birds and need their sleep. They are not going to be going out late at night very often.

You'll get bored of your Rat's views, mainly because you don't tend to have strong views on many things yourself. While your Rat is talking, you will be getting things done.

You could take your Rat to an art gallery or a museum because you are both into art and history. That will make you both happy for one night.

THE LOWE DOWN

You're not going to want to take this anywhere after the first date. Your Rat will drive you mad wanting to hit the town until very late and with their constant opinions on everything.

Verdict: AVOID

Rooster and Ox

This is one of those perfect matches. Oxen are the homemakers and you will go out and make the dosh.

You and your Ox will share many beliefs in life, kindness being just one of them. You will both go out of your way to help others and there will always be an extra place laid at your dinner table in case someone drops around.

You will be happy on a dog walking date. I can even see the two of you using an app that allows you to walk other people's dogs.

THE LOWE DOWN

There is great balance in this mix. It really could go the distance.

Verdict: DATE, LOVE, MARRY

Rooster and Tiger

Okay so you can date, and it will be fun, but this is not a long-term relationship.

You are both super strong personalities. You're unlikely to make a home that you could live in together because you would spend more time out than in.

Your dates will be really diverse. You could end up being serial daters or even BFFs. I suggest taking your Tiger go-kart racing and then to a make your own pizza place.

THE LOWE DOWN

You could date a few times or end up in the friendzone, but this match is going to go the distance.

Verdict: DATE

Rooster and Rabbit

This match could be a disaster. All I can see is clash, clash and more clashing. Some opposites work and that could include you and your Rabbit.

You may not date, you may not fall in love, you may not marry, but you could end up being BFFs.

If you decide to date, then perhaps start with feeding some ducks. That will give you a chance to see if there is any possibility of a longer-term relationship with your Rabbit.

THE LOWE DOWN

You could give it a chance. I can't see it working but why don't you see what the ducks have to say?

Verdict: AVOID

Rooster and Dragon

You and your Dragon are a great match. You both bring something to the match that the other needs. You love your Dragon for their knowledge, and they really need your wild side for some fun. Added to that you are secret friends. In this case, friends with very definite benefits.

You also have a spiritual connection with your Dragon, and you could spend hours discussing your thoughts.

Okay so for a first date with your Dragon – how about trying a séance? Then you could take them off for a glass of wine to talk about what you've been told will happen in your future.

THE LOWE DOWN

This could really work – you are great friends, and you bring so much value into each other's lives.

Verdict: DATE, LOVE, MARRY

Rooster and Snake

This really is a great option. You have so much in common in both your personal and professional life. You and your Snake are really driven but you know how to have a laugh together.

You will enjoy the sparkly stuff, the fancy cars and fine dining together. I think you get the picture. You both love the finer things in life.

So, you will understand why I suggest that you take your Snake shopping followed by cocktails in a trendy bar, with low music, so you can chat. You both love to chat.

THE LOWE DOWN

This really is an excellent match and can go the distance.

Verdict: DATE, LOVE, MARRY

Rooster and Horse

This just isn't going to work on any level. Your Horse is going to try and control your playtime, activities, and emotions. Roosters, you love your freedom and have a mind of your own. If someone tries to control you, you will just turn around and show them your tail feathers.

The only date I can see working is a fencing lesson. But perhaps it's not a good idea giving you both a weapon.

THE LOWE DOWN

This isn't going to work. You will be miserable so don't go there.

Verdict: AVOID

Rooster and Goat

Roosters and Goats are part of the negotiating team of the Chinese Animals, so dating really won't work as without knowing it you could end up talking yourselves into endless knots or going around in circles.

But you do have an excellent chance of becoming great friends. I recommend taking your Goat to a gin bar followed by a quiet Italian restaurant so you can chat to your hearts' content.

THE LOWE DOWN

There's not going to be any romance, but you will have a great time.

Verdict: DATE, FRIENDZONE

Rooster and Monkey

You two will get along great. You'll become fast friends and talk for ages. It won't matter what you do, or where you do it, you'll just keep talking. You'll also make fantastic business partners.

You can go anywhere and do anything, but a pub crawl with a kebab afterwards would work for both of you.

THE LOWE DOWN

You're going to have a great time together but you're more than likely to end up great friends.

Verdict: DATE, FRIENDZONE

Rooster and Rooster

Imagine this – the two of you on a date competing for 'mirror time'. You'll both be preening and looking at yourselves too much for this to get off the ground.

I wouldn't bother going on a date, but if you do, I can hear Carly Simon singing, "You're so vain…" in the background.

THE LOWE DOWN

Nope, this is really not going to work.

Verdict: AVOID

Rooster and Dog

This is not great, really not great. You're going to argue, make each other feel insecure and then you'll be crowing, and your Dog will be barking loudly.

You won't make beautiful music together – it will just be noise and not happy noise.

No date. Unless you can find one of those soundproofed rooms where no one else can hear you argue.

THE LOWE DOWN

No, no and no!

Verdict: AVOID

Rooster and Pig

Roosters and Pigs have a strange relationship. You want to get it on but the fact that you both need your own space will get in the way.

Your Pig will try to dominate the relationship as it can become jealous of any outside influences. That could lead to you looking elsewhere for company.

You both smell amazing. Anyone walking past either of you will chase after you to find out what perfume or aftershave you are wearing.

An unusual date that would work for you and your Pig would be a day making your own perfume.

THE LOWE DOWN

You will have fun, no doubt, but it's not going anywhere.

Verdict: DATE, FRIENDZONE

THE LOWE DOWN

DATE:

LOVE:

MARRY:

AVOID:

SPECIAL MENTIONS:

Friendzone

Did you know...?

Some of the world's most prominent leaders in their fields have been Roosters including Aung San Suu Kyi, Ruth Bader Ginsburg and John Glenn.

A surprising number of sports stars are Roosters such as Anna Kournikova, Serena Williams, Zara Phillips, Jayne Torvill, Steffi Graf and Shane Warne.

Some of the more flamboyant dressers amongst Roosters are Dolly Parton, Harry Styles and Beyoncé Knowles.

Roosters don't always get along with other Roosters. They tend to take time to size each other up.

Dog

The eleventh sign in the Chinese zodiac is Dog.

At first sight:

Dog years	You were born after the Chinese New Year in: 1912, 1924, 1936, 1958, 1970, 1982, 1994, 2006 or, if you are very young, 2018.
Dog months	Your love mojo is going to be highest in February, June and October. From 7th November to 6th December, you are going to be on fire!
Dog days	Dust off your best dating gear on Thursdays.
Dog hours	As a night owl you are hottest between 7pm and 1am.
Element	Earth

Top traits	Faithful, loyal, and protective like its namesake, a Dog. They can be cautious and take a while to make the right decision but when they know they know.
How you're likely to appear on your first date	Probably in a pub over a pint... they are not the most romantic – a little bit more conservative.
Best colours	You'll rock red, orange and purple but ditch grey it will kill the mood.
Lucky number	Your best number is 6 but 4 just isn't going to work for you.
Lucky direction	Happy days your best directions are Northeast, East & South. Southeast isn't the direction you want to be heading.

Dogs are extremely loyal and will have your back in any situation if you are their friends.

You are super strong-willed and, if you're not careful, you can come across stubborn or a bit controlling. Your way isn't always right, even though you may think it is. Part of your stubbornness is because you're unsure that people can see both sides of a situation and, honestly, you're not a great fan of change. Change is difficult for you. You don't make hasty decisions. For example, if you're booking a holiday, you would investigate the hotel, flights, and the price, and then you would check it all again to make sure it's the best possible deal. There is nothing wrong with that, but your procrastination may make others a little bored, and they may go and find another holiday without you.

You are the most reliable and trustworthy of the Chinese animal signs.

At school you may have been at your most studious with subjects like maths and geography capturing your attention. You would also have loved sport like hockey, football, netball – basically anything with a ball.

It will come as no surprise to you that you need to be around people. You're a social soul and you'll often be found in pubs, restaurants, sports events and music festivals.

You have a love of food and, perhaps, wine. You'll surround yourself with people who love to be around food, and will love sharing a vintage bottle of red. You love to entertain and show off your culinary skills. You may have several cookbooks and love working with a recipe although you've been known to throw your own extra ingredient in which can sometimes lead to success and sometimes a culinary disaster.

When looking for a partner you should look for someone with a similar social life as yours.

Home is only somewhere you'll go if there's nothing else going on or you fancy catching up with stamp collecting or knitting.

Dogs are introverted, but quietly, very opinionated. You're not particularly sensitive although you can be emotional.

Are you intuitive? You could be if you took your head out of what is expected to be the norm! When you're around intuitive people you will start to see how you tap into your own thoughts and realise that everything isn't as black and white as you thought it was.

Dogs' homes are messy, and you have a tendency to keep everything, to the extent of becoming hoarders with overly cluttered homes. If you have visitors coming over, you rush around with the hoover and duster.

You prefer being outdoors, but fitness isn't high on your agenda. You want to be fit but it takes a lot of effort and you'd rather be socialising. If you need to exercise it will need to be outside and the gym is not your chosen place.

Dogs can be stay-at-home parents or career types. You're likely to find that you're much more suited to 9 to 5 jobs so you have time to enjoy your social life and outside interests. You're really suited to any planning-oriented jobs or working with figures. You'd make great nurses and doctors, but the shift work would mess with your work/life balance and desire to socialise. Finding a job in entertaining or one that involves regular entertainment or socialising would work perfectly.

You will hate any job that requires selling, and your weakness could be in over promising and under delivering. But your superpower is in putting systems into place and being methodical.

Dogs can scrub up well and look super smart for special occasions, but casualwear suits you best. You are very yin and yang when it comes to fast cars and fancy gear. If you couldn't have it all you would always choose to spend it on your hobbies like golf and travel first. You do like to buy branded clothing.

Let's talk about love…

Dogs are happy being single but prefer to be in relationships. Dogs don't run into a relationship even though it's their preference. You take your time, and your choice isn't always from the heart, it's also about your head.

You can be a little anxious and a bit pessimistic and don't like spending time by yourself, so partnerships are important to you. If you're not in a relationship, you can feel a bit lost.

You can take a long time to make your mind up about the right partner but once you find them then you are extremely loyal, reliable, and trustworthy. One-night stands are a definite possibility before you meet your perfect match. You're not really into PDAs or even particularly cuddly.

Dogs can find partners for life, but you can also find yourself getting married a few times. You may have kids, but you will still want to have a social life and children will be brought up to adapt. You will be a loving parent.

In a partner you want someone who isn't selfish and will be supportive of you and your ideas. Someone who likes outdoor sports and pubs will be a huge bonus.

Less than surprisingly your favourite dates will be in pubs, but curry houses and anywhere with food and alcohol will work well for you. Your date can expect you to be late but with a good excuse. You can be organised with dating but from the outside you will look disorganised. You'll be smartly dressed for the occasion, but people will only get your attention if you like them, or they chat about things you're interested in. You'll probably take a bit of time before you warm up to them. You'll need to know someone a bit better before you make a move.

You're a late-night person. Early mornings are not your scene unless you have something fun planned. Then you'll drag yourself out of bed.

So, let's get down to business and tell you which signs in the Chinese Horoscopes you should date, love, marry or avoid.

Let's talk about love...

Dog and Rat

You are poles apart but will make good friends. You would struggle dating your Rat because Rats tend to go with the flow, and you will want to be methodical.

You like to talk about sport and about trips abroad, whereas your Rat will inevitably be into politics, social issues or how they can save the planet.

If you decide to give it a go, I suggest a pizza and a bottle of red on a picnic in the park.

THE LOWE DOWN

This is going nowhere except friendship.

Verdict: FRIENDZONE

Dog and Ox

You two have the same principles in life. You are loyal, trustworthy and kind. Both of you are quiet serious animals. Your Ox is a loving homemaker whereas you will prefer your home to be set up for you. Both of you love being outside in fresh air.

Sadly, neither of you will bring the fun into this match and you both really need it.

You are much more suited to be friends, but if you want to try a date perhaps treat your Ox to coffee and cake. You might have a friend more suited to your Ox and vice versa, so you **could use the time for some matchmaking instead.**

THE LOWE DOWN

Strictly friendship. Nothing to see here.

Verdict: FRIENDZONE

Dog and Tiger

Oh yes, this relationship can go for the long haul. You have so much in common. Your Tiger will bring the fun to the table, and you will be the level-headed one keeping their feet on the ground.

Your Tiger will go out and make money and you will be responsible for the spreadsheets and organisation behind the scenes.

Your Tiger can be rash, but you will take your time with decisions. So, you sound like you are opposites but actually you really complement each other.

Given you and your Tiger love being outside – why not take them camping with only one tent. Let's be honest, you're going to end up in bed anyway. So, start as you mean to go on.

THE LOWE DOWN

This one can go all the way if you want it to.

Verdict: DATE, LOVE, MARRY

Dog and Rabbit

You and your Rabbit will get along. You both like to do your own thing, so you understand each other's need for space. This will make for a balanced relationship.

You bring loyalty to the relationship and your Rabbit brings trust. That will ensure that you can both relax around each other, knowing that when you marry (yes, I did say marry!) you will have each other's back.

I suggest you start off your date with breakfast where you can plan your day together.

THE LOWE DOWN

Yes, this match can work well for both of you.

Verdict: DATE, LOVE, MARRY

Dog and Dragon

You two will argue, argue some more and then have a good row. The only upside to this relationship is that people passionate enough to argue are often those who really like making up again.

But in truth I would give this match a wide berth. If you decide you want to try it out, then a great date option would be paintballing because you can take out your frustration with each other in a fun way.

THE LOWE DOWN

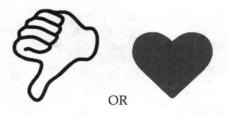

OR

You can definitely date, fall in love and even marry if you like very tempestuous relationships and a lot of drama. But if you want peace then avoid!

Verdict: AVOID OR LOVE, DATE, MARRY?

Dog and Snake

There will be a lot of flirting between you and your Snake. Your Snake will hypnotise, and you will charm. You will fall for your Snake and that's when it will all start to go wrong.

Ultimately your Snake will start to get bored with you. The only possible date I can think of is sitting a maths test together, because you are both great with figures. Yep – that really is the best I can do with this match!

THE LOWE DOWN

Have your date – you'll love all the flirting. But stick to being friends after that.

Verdict: DATE, FRIENDZONE

Dog and Horse

You two have so much in common that you will make much better friends than lovers. Your love of travel will bond you together. You're both headstrong so that does mean a few arguments are likely to arise.

This match will stay in the friendzone because there really is no passion between you.

You will be great friends though. Because you both love to travel I'd suggest a riverboat cruise at night.

THE LOWE DOWN

No spark here but you will stay great friends.

Verdict: DATE, FRIENDZONE

Dog and Goat

This really is a match made in hell. You're both so stubborn that you won't even bother to argue, you'll just sulk to get your point across.

I wouldn't bother with a date but if you must then go to a class where you can role play, and both pretend to be someone else.

THE LOWE DOWN

Definitely avoid. This will never work.

Verdict: AVOID

Dog and Monkey

This is a match! Whoop whoop!!! I would say to just jump straight into bed, but you're a cautious animal and take time to warm up to people, so perhaps do that after a few drinks.

You will want to impress your Monkey so take them somewhere sophisticated. Think a tux and sparkling dresses, or High Tea at the Savoy. You love the finer things in life so show your Monkey a great time.

THE LOWE DOWN

There is every chance that this match will work well.

Verdict: DATE, LOVE, MARRY

Dog and Rooster

No! This match is not going to work. You are mesmerised by the Rooster, but the Rooster just isn't going to be interested.

You will have so many opposing views on life that you will bicker about literally everything. You want to control everything, and your Rooster just turns its back and walks off in the opposite direction, which will infuriate you.

If you still want to go on a date after reading this, then perhaps try couple's yoga.

THE LOWE DOWN

I can't even see the point in dating your Rooster, it's just not going to work.

Verdict: AVOID

Dog and Dog

I just want to yawn when I think of this match. Yes, you do both like the same things, but your relationship would be boring.

There's just not going to be any fire. If you want to try a date despite the lack of va va voom, then there is a possibility you could end up friends, someone you could call on if you have an extra ticket for Wimbledon.

If you're looking for a date option, then perhaps involve a kayak or a canoe followed by a picnic with a lot of cheese.

THE LOWE DOWN

You'll enjoy your date, but nothing is going to happen here.

Verdict: DATE

Dog and Pig

You and your Pig come together bonding on trust and kindness. Work is important to both of you. At the end of the working day, you'll share your experiences over a bottle of the best red wine.

Given your love of the great outdoors I suggest a wine tour, where you can walk hand in hand through the vineyard and then share a great bottle of wine, your shared favourite thing to do.

THE LOWE DOWN

This could go the distance.

Verdict: DATE, LOVE, MARRY

THE LOWE DOWN

DATE:

LOVE:

MARRY:

AVOID:

SPECIAL MENTIONS:

Friendzone

Did you know...?

A number of political leaders are Dogs – Bill Clinton, Yitzhak Rabin, Boutros Boutros-Ghali and George W. Bush.

Some Dogs have changed the world like Mother Teresa.

A few Dogs have well and truly taken the wrong turn in life including Ted Bundy and Charles Manson.

Some Dogs have influenced fashion in a big way like Gianni Versace and Giorgio Armani.

Dogs that have reached the top of their chosen field are Yuri Gagarin, Judi Dench, Maggie Smith, Steven Spielberg, Freddie Mercury, David Bowie, Madonna, Queen Latifah, Elvis Presley, and Leonard Cohen.

Roosters can tend to be controversial characters like Britney Spears, Prince Philip and Ellen DeGeneres.

You can see the reliability of a Dog in people like Prince William.

Pig

The twelfth and final animal sign in the Chinese Horoscope is the Pig.

At first sight:

Pig years	You were born after the Chinese New Year in: 1923, 1935, 1947, 1959, 1971, 1983, 1995, 2007 or, if you are very young, 2019.
Pig months	Your love mojo is going to be highest in November and July. You are on Fire 4th February through to 4th April.
Pig days	Dust off your best dating gear on Saturdays.
Pig hours	Early bird, you can wake as early as 3am.
Element	Water
Top traits	Logical, honest, good-natured and love to have fun, but on a serious note they have great empathy.
How you're likely to appear on your first date	Can wear a smart suit but happiest in a pair of jeans with a shirt or T-shirt.

Best colours	You'll rock blue, white, black and grey, but ditch the red it will kill the mood.
Lucky number	Your best number is 1, but 3 just isn't going to work for you.
Lucky direction	Happy days, your best directions are Northwest, Southwest, and Northeast. Southeast isn't the direction you want to be heading.

Let's talk a bit about you. You are someone who takes your obligations very seriously, personally and professionally. It's important to you that everything is correct and in its place.

There is more than a touch of OCD about you. You will notice this in so many ways in your life. You probably wear the same clothes every day, and may even be happy to wear a uniform, so you don't have to get up and worry about what you're going to put on.

Anyone in your life who doesn't expect complete honesty is going to get a surprise. You are honest to a fault. But alongside that you are really good-natured and really don't like people who argue or don't get on. You are often the person who brings calm to a situation where others are running around tearing their hair out. You see the answers to most situations before others even know what is going to happen. This is where you draw on your intuition. Do you think you're intuitive? Yes of course, you know you are. It's gotten you out of a few fixes.

You know that you are super fussy picking your friends and anyone who is counted in that number knows that it's a huge honour. You do not like fools, and you can't deal with ill-mannered people. Do unto others as they do unto you is not one of your beliefs. You would rather just walk away from people who aren't worth your energy.

Indulgence is a feature in your life. While you're happy to spend money on yourself you will always make sure the people around you don't go without. Those around you will fall in love with your heart and kindness. Others will fall in love with your mind. Your intelligence is one of your superpowers.

You are super creative in business and have the knack of forging business relationships which make you extremely valuable to organisations. You are a very attractive option for companies who want to lead the world in their sector and need creative types in their teams.

In investments you are shrewd and will do all your homework before you consider putting your money anywhere. You've got the knack of knowing when to invest for the long haul in options others might think are fads.

Although you think you're an introvert, you are actually an extrovert. That said, being in your own space and having a bit of solitude is very important to you. However, the way you are around your friends they will never guess that. You've got a lot of opinions, and while you're not afraid to share them, you do it in a way that doesn't upset people.

At school you would be serious about technical subjects like IT and love history, but very easily distracted if you weren't interested in the subject matter, especially if wasn't going to contribute to your future career. You were a rule breaker and detention may well have been in your past. You don't mind taking the part of the class clown.

In your younger years you are a party animal but when you settle into a relationship then your spare time is more couple-oriented. Rock and roll is very much your thing in your teens and twenties but once you get into a relationship a lot of that will stop. You are a lover of food and wine, and it would be very unlike you to eat or drink anything boring; you love spicy food and when travelling the world, you will try the local food.

At night you're a homebody and generally early to bed. You're an early bird by nature, so while you can and will party in your younger years, your natural rhythm is to go to bed and get up early.

Pigs are lucky in love, but you don't just fall in love with random people. You know exactly what you're looking for. PDAs are definitely on the menu with the right partner. Pigs prefer to be in relationships, but only with the right person. However, Pigs aren't often alone because people can't help but fall in love with you. The right person for you is going to have ambition but will love snuggling up and watching a boxset with you.

Marriage is an odd one with Pigs. You may not want to get married until later in life. You like being in a relationship, but marriage can feel a bit like a trap to you. BUT, and it's a big but, that doesn't mean you aren't happy to commit to the right person forever. Kids are not a given with Pigs, you can choose to have them or not, but if you do you will make a great parent.

Pigs choose minimalism if they have a choice, they really hate clutter. With fashion you are into your brands, however, it's more about the quality. You'll have an individual style and will always look smart. You don't mind dressing up, in fact, you love it. You love your fancy cars and there's not much chance of finding any self-respecting Pig in a practical option.

Are you more likely to be into your career or a home type? You're into both, but most of you will want a career alongside your home life. Pigs make great accountants, lawyers, historians, researchers and do really well in IT, healthcare and artificial intelligence. Whatever you choose it must be interesting and set your mind on fire. Something dull or that doesn't grab you is just not going to work.

You're an overly sensitive soul but the silver lining is that you are intuitive. In fact, your superpowers include your intuition; you know everything and you're skilled at placing people in the right job within a company.

You are not good with authority or being told what to do. In your younger years you would let your parents tell you what to do and then go your own way. So, when looking for a job ensure that you get on with your boss in the interview; if you don't then this isn't the job for you.

Fitness is important to you both internally and physically, you know which vitamins to take and will investigate new products on the market. You love the gym unlike others, because you like routine. So, running on the treadmill and listening to podcasts makes you happy.

Let's talk about love...

You need loyalty in a love partner. They must be completely honest, and they must never lie. Once your trust has gone the relationship is over. You want someone you can build a home with who shares your love of fun and adventure. Pigs have no tolerance for stupid people, so you need someone who is intelligent.

Perfect dates for Pigs are historical houses and exhibitions. Anywhere you can indulge your love of fine food and wine will be a winner. Long walks in the woods and aquariums are other places you'll enjoy. You will always be on time or early for dates and they will be uber-organised.

Your date can expect you to be on time, dressed to impress and you'll smell divine. You'll be flirty, but you'll be sussing them out at the same time. They can expect to laugh a lot and be the focus of your attention, if they match up to your exacting standards.

One-night stands are not out of the question, but never when you're in a relationship. Once you find your love partner you will be absolutely loyal and faithful.

So, let's get down to business and tell you which signs in the Chinese Horoscopes you should date, love, marry or avoid.

Let's talk about love…

Pig and Rat

You two have something magical between you. It might even feel like you met in a previous life. You both have a love of travel, family, music and… oh the list is endless!

Although saying that, you do like a bit of time on your own, but you'll respect each other's time out.

I suggest a date with a mix of culture, fun and then some smoochy time alone. You could take your Rat to visit Madame Tussauds, hit a fun bar, then find an Italian restaurant off the beaten track that serves the yummiest spaghetti bolognese.

THE LOWE DOWN

You two can take this the whole way. The trick is for your Rat to know when to give you time by yourself and to stop talking.

Verdict: DATE, LOVE, MARRY

Pig and Ox

Pigs can spend a lot of time looking out of the window, leading a solitary life. You're not lonely but you can find yourself alone a lot. Your Ox will ground you and bring you out of your comfortable solitude.

Oxen are masters at making warm, welcoming, comfortable homes, and you will show your Ox how to have a good time.

Food is really important to you and your Ox. You both like to experiment so a date with a cookery experience would suit you and your Ox. Perhaps Venetian cuisine with accompanying Bellinis would whet your appetite, especially if you get to eat it later.

THE LOWE DOWN

Marriage is a definite possibility for you two. You balance each other out.

Verdict: DATE, LOVE, MARRY

Pig and Tiger

Tigers can be your BFFs. So, can you wind up in the friendzone? Oh no – not you two. The passion and sexual attraction fizzing between you both will make sure that never happens.

An intimate dinner for two somewhere with good food and wine will provide the precursor for the 'dessert'.

THE LOWE DOWN

Is this marriage material? Oh yes, it is! What's better than a bestie you fancy like mad? You two can go all the way.

Verdict: DATE, LOVE, MARRY

Pig and Rabbit

This one has serious potential so you can invest in an exciting date with your Rabbit. You and your Rabbit are a definite possibility. You bring the trust and your Rabbit will bring the love.

I suggest whisking your Rabbit away for a weekend abroad. Anywhere with sea, wine and your phones handy to keep in touch with family, and you will both be happy.

A romantic trip to Paris is a great option. Take the train so you can enjoy the view.

THE LOWE DOWN

Yes! This one can go all the way.

Verdict: MARRY, MARRY, MARRY

Pig and Dragon

You and your Dragon are going to connect on an intellectual level. You'll find each other interesting and will love debating a range of different subjects. Your Dragon will be as up to date with world news as you are.

You are both kind and help wherever you can. You'll both make donations to charities but not tell anyone except, perhaps, each other.

A date that will really impress your Dragon would be a charity event.

THE LOWE DOWN

Your brains will be attracted to each other, and you will both be stimulated by your date BUT not in the way you need for an ongoing relationship.

Verdict: DATE, FRIENDZONE

Pig and Snake

When I think of this match, I foresee fireworks and not the fun, celebratory ones. You and your Snake are going to clash massively. You are far too similar for it to work. If one of you put a plate in the wrong cupboard your nerves would shatter, a bit like Monica in *Friends*.

Literally the only date option I can think of is to go straight to relationship counselling to save time.

THE LOWE DOWN

Give it a miss!

Verdict: AVOID

Pig and Horse

This is a match that has the intellectual stimulation and the sexy kind needed for a relationship. You both have business brains and you're into figures (as in sums).

You both have a passion for life. Neither of you want to miss a minute without filling it with things to do.

I can see you both at a self-development conference to improve yourselves or your lives. You both like the finer things in life so you and your Horse will love great food and wine, so perhaps dinner afterwards to talk about the conference.

THE LOWE DOWN

Verdict: DATE, LOVE, MARRY

Emma Thompson (Pig) and hubby Greg Wise (Horse) have found their match.

Pig and Goat

You two will be great friends and this is one friendship that can definitely turn into marriage. You'll be the boss and make most of the decisions. Your Goat's kind nature will allow them to bend to your will.

I suggest a date at an art gallery or museum followed by some sushi.

THE LOWE DOWN

This is one time when friendship can grow into a lasting love. You could be taking your Goat down the aisle.

Verdict: DATE, LOVE, MARRY

Pig and Monkey

There is no point dating each other. Monkeys are cheeky and you will just get on each other's nerves. Chances are you will both see each other as fake. Monkeys will just send you back into yourself and you'll come across as aloof.

A date sitting in a library where you can't talk to each other but can find a good book to read. I think you get the picture.

THE LOWE DOWN

You two will just bring the worst out in each other. Give it a miss.

Verdict: AVOID

Pig and Rooster

Both of you are creative animals, one of you could be an artist and the other into IT. You really appreciate each other's qualities and have a respect for your different life journeys.

You can be a bit jealous, because you don't like to share your partners. You know they need to have friends, but you prefer them home early and tucked up in bed next to you. While your Rooster is more than happy to come home early, they won't like any sense of being controlled.

This isn't really going to work, but if you decide to take your Rooster out then try a day at the races.

THE LOWE DOWN

Dating will be fun. It could possibility end in marriage, or you could stay friends.

Verdict: DATE, FRIENDZONE (POSSIBLY MARRIAGE)

Pig and Dog

You are both hard workers and career comes first for you and your Dog. Both of you know how to put a PowerPoint presentation and spreadsheet together.

That said, if you decide to marry, you'll both love putting your house together. That's not to say there won't be a few cross words because you are a minimalist, and your Dog is prone to just adding a picture or ornament somewhere randomly. However, as you're both kind by nature this won't be a big problem.

My date suggestion is to take a hot air balloon ride – it will be a great mix of slightly risky and great fun.

THE LOWE DOWN

A meeting of two clever minds and building trust is a great recipe for marriage. This can go all of the way.

Verdict: DATE, LOVE, MARRY

Pig and Pig

A date between two Pigs will be like an OCD support group. You'll probably wind up updating your LinkedIn profiles together over a mocha, choca, almond milk coffee. You are both super intelligent and could really enjoy each other's company and understand each other's OCD quirks.

By all means find a great café and treat your Pig to a fancy coffee but too much of anything is not great. Two Pigs in a relationship is OCD on overdrive.

THE LOWE DOWN

This is not a match made in heaven. You will stimulate each other's brain but also trigger each other's OCD traits. A date or two is fine but this really isn't going anywhere great.

Verdict: DATE, FRIENDZONE

THE DOWN LOWE

DATE:

LOVE:

Pig

MARRY:

AVOID:

SPECIAL MENTIONS:

Friendzone

Did you know...?

Pigs can be leaders in every form of life like the 14th Dalai Lama (Tenzin Gyatso), Ronald Reagan, Hillary Clinton and Mike Pence.

Some Pigs have reached the top of their fields including Elon Musk, Elton John, Luciano Pavarotti and Stephen King.

It would be easier to name the actors who weren't born Pigs but some of those are Glenn Close, David Tennant, Chris Hemsworth, Emma Thompson, Lucille Ball, Ginger Rogers, Sandra Oh and Jada Pinkett Smith.

Pigs can be very musical souls and some of them are Bryan Adams, Amy Winehouse, Michael Hutchence, Dido, Iggy Pop, Richie Sambora and Ricky Martin.

Some Pigs who have made their struggle with 'authority' known or who have fallen foul of it are Julian Assange and John McEnroe. In very different ways they have challenged the powers that be.

Alice Cooper, Iggy Pop and Richie Sambora are only a few of the Pigs who really enjoyed the rock and roll, party lifestyle in their younger years.

In conclusion...

I love you the more in that I believe you had liked me for my own sake and for nothing else.

– John Keats

Human beings need to connect with one another. We are fundamentally social beings and most of you reading this book will know that the often-repeated phrase, "No man is an island," (John Donne) is as true as it ever was.

No. The fact is that if we want to talk about islands – we want to be on that island with someone we love, or at least fancy like crazy.

In our modern world with technology and busy, busy lives, meeting someone you want to date, let alone love or marry has become an art form. Most of us are too busy to be kissing a lot of those proverbial frogs. We want to focus our efforts on the Chinese animals with more potential.

So, whether you're looking for a bit of extracurricular activity, or a lifelong partner to have a family with, a bit of help is welcome for all of us. We live in a world where time is the most in-demand commodity so a little bit of help to work out who our most compatible partners are is likely to be a huge benefit.

I loved writing *Love, Date, Marry, Avoid* and I hope that the insight and knowledge in it helps you find your happy ever after, if that's what you're looking for.

I'd love to get your feedback on the book.

You can find me at: https://www.janinelowe.co.uk/

Previous Title

Manifest Journal for Inspirational People
ISBN 979-8710613566

O-BOOKS

SPIRITUALITY

O is a symbol of the world, of oneness and unity; this eye represents knowledge and insight. We publish titles on general spirituality and living a spiritual life. We aim to inform and help you on your own journey in this life.

If you have enjoyed this book, why not tell other readers by posting a review on your preferred book site?

Recent bestsellers from O-Books are:

Heart of Tantric Sex
Diana Richardson
Revealing Eastern secrets of deep love and intimacy to Western couples.
Paperback: 978-1-90381-637-0 ebook: 978-1-84694-637-0

Crystal Prescriptions
The A-Z guide to over 1,200 symptoms and their healing crystals
Judy Hall
The first in the popular series of eight books, this handy little guide is packed as tight as a pill-bottle with crystal remedies for ailments.
Paperback: 978-1-90504-740-6 ebook: 978-1-84694-629-5

Your Simple Path
Find Happiness in every step
Ian Tucker
A guide to helping us reconnect with what is really important in our lives.
Paperback: 978-1-78279-349-6 ebook: 978-1-78279-348-9

365 Days of Wisdom
Daily Messages To Inspire You Through The Year
Dadi Janki
Daily messages which cool the mind, warm the heart and guide you along your journey.
Paperback: 978-1-84694-863-3 ebook: 978-1-84694-864-0

Body of Wisdom
Women's Spiritual Power and How it Serves
Hilary Hart
Bringing together the dreams and experiences of women across the world with today's most visionary spiritual teachers.
Paperback: 978-1-78099-696-7 ebook: 978-1-78099-695-0

Dying to Be Free
From Enforced Secrecy to Near Death to True Transformation
Hannah Robinson
After an unexpected accident and near-death experience, Hannah Robinson found herself radically transforming her life, while a remarkable new insight altered her relationship with her father, a practising Catholic priest.
Paperback: 978-1-78535-254-6 ebook: 978-1-78535-255-3

The Ecology of the Soul
A Manual of Peace, Power and Personal Growth for Real People
in the Real World
Aidan Walker
Balance your own inner Ecology of the Soul to regain your
natural state of peace, power and wellbeing.
Paperback: 978-1-78279-850-7 ebook: 978-1-78279-849-1

Not I, Not other than I
The Life and Teachings of Russel Williams
Steve Taylor, Russel Williams
The miraculous life and inspiring teachings of one of the World's
greatest living Sages.
Paperback: 978-1-78279-729-6 ebook: 978-1-78279-728-9

On the Other Side of Love
A woman's unconventional journey towards wisdom
Muriel Maufroy
When life has lost all meaning, what do you do?
Paperback: 978-1-78535-281-2 ebook: 978-1-78535-282-9

Practicing A Course In Miracles
A translation of the Workbook in plain language, with
mentor's notes
Elizabeth A. Cronkhite
The practical second and third volumes of The Plain-Language
A Course In Miracles.
Paperback: 978-1-84694-403-1 ebook: 978-1-78099-072-9

Quantum Bliss

The Quantum Mechanics of Happiness, Abundance, and Health

George S. Mentz

Quantum Bliss is the breakthrough summary of success and spirituality secrets that customers have been waiting for.

Paperback: 978-1-78535-203-4 ebook: 978-1-78535-204-1

The Upside Down Mountain

Mags MacKean

A must-read for anyone weary of chasing success and happiness – one woman's inspirational journey swapping the uphill slog for the downhill slope.

Paperback: 978-1-78535-171-6 ebook: 978-1-78535-172-3

Your Personal Tuning Fork

The Endocrine System

Deborah Bates

Discover your body's health secret, the endocrine system, and 'twang' your way to sustainable health!

Paperback: 978-1-84694-503-8 ebook: 978-1-78099-697-4

Readers of ebooks can buy or view any of these bestsellers by clicking on the live link in the title. Most titles are published in paperback and as an ebook. Paperbacks are available in traditional bookshops. Both print and ebook formats are available online.

Find more titles and sign up to our readers' newsletter at http://www.johnhuntpublishing.com/mind-body-spirit

Follow us on Facebook at https://www.facebook.com/OBooks/ and Twitter at https://twitter.com/obooks